Nobody's Child Anymore

1/01

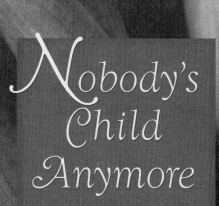

Nobody's Child Anymore

Grieving, Caring, and Comforting When Parents Die

Barbara Bartocci

SORIN BOOKS   Notre Dame, IN

© 2000 by Sorin Books

All rights reserved. No part of this book may be used or reproduced in any manner whatsoever except in the case of reprints in the context of reviews, without written permission from Sorin Books, P.O. Box 1006, Notre Dame, IN 46556-1006.

International Standard Book Number: 1-893732-21-5

Library of Congress Catalog Card Number: 00-102081

Cover and text design by Katherine Robinson Coleman

Printed and bound in the United States of America.

Dedicated to my dear friend

Tina Hacker

And my beloved aunts, Helen and Jean

To everything there is a season . . .

a time to be born and a time to die. . . .

The same destiny overtakes all. . . .

~Ecclesiastes

Contents

Introduction

*W*hen our parents die and we are adults, we're expected to say, "This is an appropriate death. My father . . . my mother . . . lived a full life. It is their time. I'm okay with that."
But we are not okay with it.
Losing a parent—at any age—is a profound loss.

It is such a primal connection, that of parent and child. No matter what your age, no matter what the circumstances of your rearing, no matter how loving or how lethal your relationship, it's impossible to completely ignore the people who gave you life. You can divorce a spouse but not your parents. There is that ultimate tie—the genetic inheritance that somehow entwines us no matter how hard we may try to disconnect.

As society ages, and more people experience this inevitable passage, people are beginning to realize that it's not an easy loss just because your parents are in their 60s, 70s, 80s, or even 90s.

I was surprised at the depth of my pain when my parents died. And since there isn't yet a lot of cultural support when adults lose their parents, I had to feel my way, as if walking through an unfamiliar forest.

I have written this book as a gentle guide through the forest of feelings you may be encountering. It is not a practical manual—turn to other sources for help in planning a funeral or settling an estate. Rather, I share my own experience and the thoughts and experiences of others as a source to ease your soul-pain. The four parts of this book parallel the four-fold experience of loss through which we pass. It begins when we are called upon to care for one of our parents and we come to the difficult realization that Mom or Dad is dying. Then, after the loss, we struggle with the pain of our grief and perhaps some unresolved issues in our relationship with our parents. At the same time, we are often called upon to offer comfort and support to our surviving parent. We may then lose a second parent and experience the special pain of becoming an adult "orphan." Grieving is a process that has its own time. But eventually, we come to some resolution of our pain and we complete our grief.

I have learned that there is a special light that may come in the wake of our parents' leaving. I discovered, as you will, too, that in a deeper sense, our parents don't leave us. They become part of us.

At a Loss to Help:

"My Parent is Dying"

Every once in a while, a person would tell me, "this has been the most wonderful time of my life." At best, [dying can be] not just an ending but a kind of culmination.

~IRA BYOCK, M.D.
PRESIDENT OF THE AMERICAN ACADEMY OF
HOSPICE AND PALLIATIVE MEDICINE

The Unexpected

The hospital room percolated softly with the hum of the respirator. It sounded like a coffeepot instead of a machine keeping my father alive. Carefully, I stepped around the other life-support machines, pushed aside an IV bag, and gently touched my father's face. "How is he?"

"Blood pressure has dropped," said Polly, the night nurse. She glanced at her thick charts, as if hoping to find something she'd missed. "Otherwise, no real change, I'm afraid."

"Daddy, it's me," I pleaded. "Can you open your eyes? Please? For me?"

But his face, so yellow, stayed empty and closed. Only the furrows of pain seemed to deepen.

It should have been simple surgery. A heart bypass is not unusual these days. We telephoned Daddy the night before, all his children and grandchildren. My son Andy said, "You're gonna be out of surgery at two thirty, Granddaddy? That's great. I'll call you at three."

His grandfather's hearty chuckle had spun across the telephone wires. "What do you think this is, a little Novocain job?" He was still laughing, repeating the story to the anesthesiologist, as they wheeled him into the operating room. Maybe he wouldn't be talking by three, his laughter seemed to say, but he sure expected to feel good soon. He sure didn't plan on a heart attack during surgery.

A STEP FORWARD

*M*aybe it happened in a similar way for you. A problem during surgery. Or a doctor's stunning diagnosis. Or a police officer's call: "There's been an accident. . . ." Right in the middle of ordinary living, while you're making plans for summer vacation, raising a family, going to work—abruptly, you face your parent's mortality. Sooner rather than later. Reality is so shocking, you feel it physically. You can't take it in. There is no way to cushion the blow. Even as you gasp from the pain, realize you are starting a process that is a natural part of living—the inevitable letting go of someone you love. All you can do—and what you must do—is feel the pain.

Suddenly Vulnerable

*M*y father always seemed larger than life. Indestructible. In my childhood he had skills no one else in our family possessed. He knew how to fix a car engine and how to cook chili with "secret" ingredients. He understood mysterious truths, and could answer questions like, "What is physics all about?" and "How many stars are in the sky?" But in the hospital's intensive care unit, my tall, sturdy father with his football player shoulders, lay helpless on a gurney. How could my larger-than-life dad have become so vulnerable? As I stood at my father's bedside, I raged at my inability to *do* something.

Gradually, though, memories stirred. I recalled how at the age of ten, I fell and broke my arm. Though my father had been standing right beside me, he couldn't stop my fall. At thirteen, I asked a boy to a Girl Scout dance and when the boy turned me down, I wept on my father's shoulder. He patted me and murmured, "Stupid kid. What does he know?" But he couldn't save me from feeling rejected. When I was twenty-nine, my husband died in a plane crash, and my father's face showed his anguished feeling of helplessness.

He felt as helpless then, I realized, as I felt now, when all I could do was hold his hand and murmur, "Daddy, I love you."

A STEP FORWARD

Just as my father lacked the power to save me from all of life's tribulation, I had to accept that I couldn't protect him. Even God, whom so many think of as Father, does not stop life's inevitable journey. What I could offer my father is what he had always offered me: love and comfort. You can do the same by holding your parent's hand and speaking from your heart. Realize there are some things you can't fix, and surrender your desire for absolute control. Be grateful you can offer love and comfort.

God's Answer

"Please, God, let Daddy live."

For three weeks I prayed the same prayer every day, and still my father hovered between life and death.

One day a greeting card arrived from my second husband back in Kansas. The cover said, *Sweetheart, you're the answer to my prayer,* and inside, *You're not what I prayed for exactly, but apparently you're the answer.* Despite my inner turmoil, I chuckled. I had given Bill that card years earlier, and the inside line had become a code phrase in our family whenever things didn't go as we hoped. One or the other of us would say, "This sure isn't what I prayed for exactly. . . ." Now, Bill had added six words to the card. *"Have faith in God's answer, Barbara."*

His words jolted me. Suddenly, I wondered if I had been praying backwards. The next morning, I sat quietly in the hospital chapel. "Dear God, I know what I would like," I prayed, "but how do I know what is the best answer for Daddy? You love him, too, so I release him into your hands. Help me accept your answer, whatever it may be."

A STEP FORWARD

Acceptance is the last stage in the grief process developed by Elisabeth Kubler-Ross. Acceptance is the willingness to let go, to become at peace with what is, and to have faith in an eternity that many believe holds more than this earthly life.

Acceptance is not easy, but it does bring peace. It is also the final stage in a *process*. Be gentle with yourself, recognizing that a process takes time, and the time will differ for each person. Do not rush the process, but be open to the unexpected answer.

Final Gift

For two more weeks, Daddy's condition wavered—up one day, down the next. Finally, my sister-in-law Eileen, a nurse, spoke gently to my mother. "Mom, he's not going to make it." I saw the awareness in my mother's eyes. "More surgery will only give him pain." Cotton balls clogged my throat. I could barely speak.

It was time to let my father go. The doctor stopped the dopamine that maintained his blood pressure. As a family, we gathered around. The nurse administered morphine. The pain lines smoothed from my father's face.

He would have hated to be a helpless invalid, I thought. But my throat hurt with unshed tears. *"Daddy,"* my heart cried, *"Don't leave us!"*

My mother leaned forward. Her voice had a different timbre, the vulnerable sound of a young girl. "Cy, do you feel better now? It doesn't hurt so much, does it?" She patted his cheek. "I fixed the brakes on the car, you know, just like you wanted."

I heard my brother's sob.

The afternoon spun slowly out. Like summertime, I thought, when I was a child and time seemed forever. Our voices drifted like currents of air as we reminisced. My father's hand felt slack in mine.

I heard a gasp, and my mother leaned forward. The green line of the heart monitor had gone straight. I squeezed my father's hand. Death surprised me in its gentleness.

A STEP FORWARD

Though I knew grief lay around the corner, my father's death brought a surprising peace. "Death is God's call to come home," wrote Joseph Cardinal Bernardin of Chicago when he was dying from cancer. He quoted the final line of the prayer of St. Francis of Assisi: "It is in dying that we are born to eternal life." If your parent is blessed with a natural death (not one unnaturally prolonged), you, too, may be surprised at the peace you feel, as if your parent has gone home.

Terminal Illness

My mother was diagnosed with terminal cancer two years after my father died. She was sixty-eight, played a mean game of golf, and if I had to describe her in just one word, I'd choose "feisty." As her only daughter, I wanted to be with her, but when I flew to southern California, I was not prepared for the woman who opened her front door to me. She looked frail. The skin hung so loosely on her shrunken frame that it reminded me of wrinkled stockings.

Once more I entered the land of the dying where life settled into a routine of medicine, pain, hopes raised, and hopes dashed. In my journal I wrote: *I feel as if we exist on an island in the middle of the ocean, and all around us is fog. The outside world seems invisible through the fog. How can my husband or my children or my mother's friends understand the peculiar island we float on? Their days are filled with the ordinary stuff of life. Ours are not.*

The waiting has become so excruciating that at times I think (scandalized at my own thoughts), "Do it, Mom. Complete your dying. Finish it." Last night I woke at 1 a.m., startled into consciousness by a dream in which my mother had died. In my dream, I felt sad, but appreciative, too, because she had not lingered. As I lay awake in the dark, I despaired, "What kind of terrible person am I to have such a dream?"

But later the visiting nurse told me that ambivalent feelings are common among people who tend a dying person. It doesn't come from a desire to hasten death, but from feelings of profound helplessness.

A STEP FORWARD

*I*f your parent is dying, it's natural to feel overwhelmed and estranged from "real life." Just knowing your feelings are normal may lighten the fog a little. Realize that others in your life cannot possibly understand what you are experiencing. Don't expect too much from them.

Don't expect too much from yourself either. For the time being, focus only on tasks that are essential. Arrange to take breaks from your care-taking duties. Fit in some physical exercise. If prayer has been a part of your daily life, incorporate it now. Be as gentle with yourself as you are with your loved one. Acknowledge your mixed desire to prolong life even as you also yearn to bring the awful waiting to an end.

"Please Take Me Home"

After seventeen days in the hospital, I was able to take Mom home. She was desperate to get out of the hospital, which had become for her a demeaning prison. Even though she was too weak to do more than walk from her bed to a rented wheel chair, she gazed eagerly out the patio window to her garden. In the afternoon, as sunlight slanted through the glass, she insisted on going through the stack of accumulated mail. As she sifted through the pile, not actually reading the letters and bills, simply handling them, she murmured over and over, "I've got to figure out what to do. How to get better."

Tears clogged my throat. Despite her brave words, I knew my mother was wrestling with the anguish of her own impending death. To *know* that there is a door you'll soon walk through; to know there is no way to turn aside, no escape, no way out; to grieve for the loss of your own body—what excruciating pain such anticipation must bring, I thought.

Later, I heard her whisper, in a wondering sort of way, "I can't imagine how I got so sick all of a sudden." I ached with my own helplessness. What could I do for her? Finally, I said, "Mom, if I fix you some supper, will you eat?"

A STEP FORWARD

Believing you have some control—whether or not you actually have it—helps a person feel better. It helped my mother to be at home where she could sort her mail and look at her garden. Look for ways to help your parent feel in control, even if it's over something as small as deciding what to eat. Don't be startled if your parent experiences anticipatory grief. Find some comfort in knowing that dying patients get a gift denied to others: a time to bring old conflicts to a close, seek forgiveness, and find the spiritual dimensions to life. Look for the gift enclosed in your loved one's dying.

Vision

My mother grew up in a large Victorian home that housed her parents, two brothers, three sisters, one grandmother, and one spinster aunt. The Second World War helped scatter the siblings but the family stayed connected, in part through my mother's frequent letters.

Now she reaped the harvest. Her two living sisters traveled hundreds of miles to stay with us

awhile. In the kitchen, where we fixed
shakes for Mom or pulverized the medica
she found so hard to swallow, my aunts told me
stories about their sister.

"Erna—your mom—never *walked* anywhere," chuckled Helen, her older sister by one
year. "She cartwheeled. She was a curly-haired
bundle of energy, always in the middle of a
crowd of friends."

"We sent Erna in to badger our mother when
we really wanted her to let us do something,"
said younger sister Jean. "Erna was like a little
bull terrier who wouldn't let go. Mother would
finally give in."

"Every summer, we spent several weeks at
an uncle's ranch outside of town," recalled
Helen. "Erna would be up at dawn to help shear
sheep. She never minded getting dirty. She was
the one who organized our hikes and picnics."

Their reminiscences helped me see my mother as the girl she had been: cartwheeling through
her childhood. I listened avidly to their stories,
hungry to know Mom in ways I never had
before.

On the days she felt better, I asked Mom my
own questions. Why did people say you were
like your grandmother? What made you fall in
love with my father? Tell me more about your
summers at the ranch. When she talked about
her childhood, I noticed Mom seemed to forget
her pain.

P FORWARD

s dying, their life story is
e final weeks, you can help
t chapter. Ask questions.
arent to tape an oral history.
v a life line on a piece to paper
ears from birth to death, and
asked her muuur to tell her about important
dates and events. What a gift if you can get to
know your parent, even a little, as the human
being who lives beyond the role of mom or dad.

Living Spirit

My mother gasped for breath. Her eyes
widened as she struggled for air. Around her, the
unit nurses worked frantically, cranking her
hospital bed upright, jerking an oxygen mask
over her nose and mouth, plunging another IV
into the Helman's lock on her thin, emaciated
arm. Yet she still struggled, her chest heaving,
her gasps ratcheting like sobs.

I had rushed Mom back to the hospital. Her
emphysema had kicked in, and now it threat-
ened to suffocate her. Dr. Tim, the oncology resident, said, "We can put her on a respirator—
though she'll never come off it—or give her morphine. But—" he paused. "The morphine could
further depress her lungs and bring on death
before morning."

I swallowed, momentarily paralyzed. Spend
whatever time she had left on a respirator? Or be
forced by an artificial breathing machine to live

longer than the rest of her body wanted? No! Mom had said more than once, "There are worse things than death, Barbara." But the other choice was so risky. I needed time to think. But there was no time, only my mother's frantic gasps. "Give her morphine," I whispered. As the morphine took hold, my mother's breathing eased. Her eyes closed. I phoned my brother Jack and he came to the hospital. We sat on each side of my mother's bed. I held her hand lightly. We were both thinking about Daddy, and our death watch with him.

But my father's face had smoothed and become peaceful. My mother's face looked angry. Frown lines furrowed her forehead. Her eyebrows seemed yanked together, and her mouth was a harsh, thin line. I remembered what Dylan Thomas wrote: "Do not go gentle into this good night." The words fit my mother. She was not going gently "She's not at peace," I murmured.

Dr. Tim stuck his head through the doorway to let us know he was going off duty.

The next hours passed slowly. I leaned my head wearily against my arm. Over and over, like a prayer, the words hummed in my head: "Mom's not ready to die yet. She's not at peace. Please, let her live."

I must have fallen asleep. Suddenly, a voice spoke. "Barbara."

"Mom! You're awake."

"Thirsty. Get me . . . a drink . . . please."

I poured her some water while Jack went for the nurse. The nurse checked her and smiled. "Her breathing is much better."

An hour later, reassured that she was out of danger, my brother and I went home. I fell into bed, exhausted.

At 8 a.m., the phone rang. Groggily, I picked it up. It was Dr. Tim.

"I just came on duty—and your mother's still alive." He sounded so astonished that, sleepy as I was, I laughed.

"It's the power of the human spirit," I said. "Mom wasn't ready to go." To myself, I added, "And maybe the power of prayer."

A STEP FORWARD

*U*rgent decisions are thrust upon caretakers of dying patients. The responsibility is heavy. If your parent has made a living will, and talked to you about his or her desires, it's easier. If not, prayerfully ask God to help you make the most loving decision you can. One that considers *all* your parent's needs. Once your decision is made, don't second guess yourself—or let others do so. You made the best decision you could given the circumstances. No one can do more.

Can We Talk?

*A*s the days wore on, I yearned to talk with my mother about her dying. I wanted to ask, "Are you frightened? Does God's grace comfort you at all? Do you wonder how we will remember you?" But those were not the questions my mother wanted to hear, so instead, I brushed her hair, patted her shoulder, held her hand, kissed her cheek, and murmured, "I love you."

One night, though, without intending to, I began to cry. Crankily, Mom said, "For heaven's sake, Barbara, why are you blubbering?" I blurted, "Because I'll miss you, Mom!" She looked past me, as if at something I couldn't see. "Well," she said. And then again, the single word, "Well." I took a breath. "Mom, is—is there anything special, a song or hymn, that you would like played at—you know—at your funeral?" She said nothing for a moment. Then, grumpily, "No dirges. Play something with a little *ooomph* to it." We both laughed. We *laughed!* How peculiar and how wonderful it seemed that we could laugh!

A STEP FORWARD

*I*t's important to honor a dying patient's choice to talk or *not* to talk about the impending death. Grief experts have found that while it helps some people to be open with their loved ones, others need to maintain a level of denial. The home health care nurse said to me, "Your mother may never admit she is dying. That is her prerogative. She knows. And you know she knows. That is enough."

Draw your parent out if it seems appropriate, but don't force your parent to talk.

Terror!

Her doctors had scheduled Mom for a surgical implant and I thought she understood why. But on the morning of surgery, when I walked into her room, my mother's eyes were *black* with terror. She was, in that moment, a terrified child whose bony hand grasped mine with awful strength. Her voice shook. "Where have you been? Why weren't you here? What are they talking about? A tube into my stomach? I don't want it! I don't want it!"

I shrank from the terror I saw. How could this be my mother? My mother was never afraid. "I can't have this tube in me!" she cried. "How will I go to luncheon with my friends?"

"It can be plugged, Mom. You won't be stuck in bed. You can go anywhere." (Knowing, even as I spoke, that she was too weak to go anywhere except bed.)

"But how long will I have this in? For five years? I'm not going to stand for something like this for five years!"

I hesitated. "Mom, you don't have five years, you know." Her face grew whiter than white. She turned to the wall. I buried my own face in my hands. I had spoken a truth she didn't want to hear.

A STEP FORWARD

To see a parent act terrified is to feel as if the very earth has moved beneath your feet, for we cling, at any age, to an absurd belief that our parents exist to keep *us* safe. If you blurt out something your parent doesn't want to hear, pray that your parent does not react with horror, but if it happens, be forgiving of yourself.

Look at your parent's terror as your final step in growing up, the moment when you find the strength to comfort the one who once comforted you.

Far Away

My brother Rob wiped one hand wearily across his forehead. He looked disheveled and tired. We had gone to the hospital cafeteria, and over plastic bowls of vegetarian chili, we talked about Mom. That is, we tried to talk. In a way there was so little to say. "She's sliding downhill," I said. "It's hard to watch."

"Which is harder," mused Rob, with a wry smile, "to be you, sitting beside her day after day? Or to be me, who lives too far away to be there? And feels guilty about it?"

I shrugged. "Either way, it's hard."

He spooned up chili. Around us, doctors and nurses in greens and whites, with name badges dangling, bustled in and out. A few families gathered wearily at tables. Silverware clinked. Shoes squeaked against tile. The fluorescent lights seemed too bright, the cafeteria too garish. We took our trays to the bussing table, and walked outside, grateful for the early evening darkness and some real air. "I leave to catch my plane in a couple of hours," said Rob. "I'll go sit with Mom. Why don't you take a break?"

"Sounds good," I agreed. As I made the ten-minute drive to Mom's house, I thought about what Rob had said. It was scary to be taking weeks off—possibly months—from my freelance business. Not working meant not earning. But being with my mother allowed me the illusion that I was able to do something for her. My brother felt helpless, powerless, and cut off. He flew down from Seattle every other weekend, which I knew took a toll on his family finances, but in between, he could only call, ask "How is she?" and hear, "About the same." I decided the harder role was to live far away.

A STEP FORWARD

Do you live too far away to be there every day? You are still able to send love and prayers. Wendy Murray Zoba lived a thousand miles away from her dying father, and during one of his many crises, she wrote in her journal: "What can I give him? It is only You he needs—only You can meet him where he is right now. That he would see You, even in the midst of his pain, that he could behold Your beauty in these dark moments, that is my deepest prayer for him now."

Prayer is powerful, and whether you live near or far, prayer is possible.

No Grandma for Katie

On his next visit, my brother brought Katie, his blue-eyed, dimpled eighteen-month-old daughter. Mom was home again, and lay on the couch in the family room, eighty pounds of bone and wrinkled skin tethered to an oxygen tank. She was happy to see Katie and said, with a weak laugh, "Katie looks like Barbara at the same age. Not much hair but a well-shaped head."

Katie toddled about the room, her small hands reaching, her bright eyes curious. She tugged at the oxygen tube that snaked through Mom's nose. Mom lifted a frail hand. "She'll never get the grandparenting we gave your children," she said to me. Her voice was sad.

"You and Granddaddy were *wonderful* grandparents," I agreed.

Then I stopped, appalled. I had spoken in the past tense. Had Mom noticed?

But she was listening to Rob as he said, "She'll never get to go out on her Granddaddy's boat."

Or go camping in their motor home, I thought. *Or hear Daddy play his harmonica and tell silly jokes. Or enjoy Mom's holiday dinners.* Rob's children were losing a precious connection with their heritage.

I turned to my mother. "You know who Katie really looks like? She looks like you."

My mother smiled. She was pleased.

A STEP FORWARD

Grandparents give something precious to a child—unconditional love, freed of day-to-day parenting rules. To lose that relationship is a great loss for you, your parent, and your child. It's appropriate to feel sad. Don't cut off the feeling.

Yet grandparents do live on—in beloved traditions ("This is Grandma's pumpkin pie recipe), in a child's smile ("Look, the baby has Granddad's mouth"), and in memories and rich family stories. A sixteenth century poet wrote, "He who is not forgotten is not dead." Let your parent know, "You will not be forgotten."

After they are gone, incorporate your deceased parents into family conversations. Let them be "Grandpa and Grandma in heaven." Hang their photographs for your kids to see. Share their history. Is it the same as a living, laughing grandmother who can hug your child? Of course not. But it is a connection.

Mom Counts!

A few days later, more complications sent Mom back to the hospital.

I was at her bedside when Dr. Tim, the oncology resident, escorted a group of interns into her room. Dr. Tim had come on duty the first day my mother was admitted, so his three months of residency paralleled her three months of in-out hospital admissions. "I'm sorry to see you back," he said, then turned to the interns. "Mrs.

Lemmon is a very special woman to her family. I applaud them for the dedication and love they show their mother."

His compliment touched me. I was happy he had noticed the attention we paid my mother. It was not accidental. I wanted her nurses to see that my mother, although terminally ill, was still a woman who mattered. Not a throwaway object. Or simply a dying old lady. She was someone who deserved their personal attention.

Another family with a parent in the oncology unit brought a photo album to the hospital. It spanned their dad's life and Sarah, the daughter, said, "The album carries the message, 'Our dad is not merely what you see here. He was Somebody in his life, someone once vigorous and strong. Be good to him.'"

Yes, I thought, as Dr. Tim squeezed my mother's hand and led his interns out, *My mother is Somebody, too.*

I was glad he had noticed.

A STEP FORWARD

*J*f your parent is in a hospital or nursing home, you can reinforce to the staff through your visits, your body language, and your inquiries that here is a person who counts. Your caring attitude will encourage theirs. If you live out of town, telephone frequently. Send cards, faxes. Do your best, near or far, to let people know your parent is still Somebody.

If You Love Me, Don't Come

While I kept watch on my dying mother, my husband Bill was putting on the finishing touches to a city-wide weekend youth camp. He was the volunteer camp chairman and I knew how hard he'd worked to make the weekend a success.

That same weekend, my mother took a turn for the worse, and for the second time, we feared she might die. I called Bill and assured him, "I just want you to know what's happening."

A few hours later, Bill called me. He was en-route to California to be with me.

I was so startled that I blurted, "But it won't help to have you here. You should have stayed at the camp."

My comment cut him deeply, and when he arrived, we had a terrible quarrel. He saw himself as heroic, a spouse who had willingly given up his beloved camp to be with his wife. But Bill and my mother did not get along. What he didn't understand was that his arrival placed added pressure on me at a time when I was struggling to hold myself together. Dealing with their conflicted relationship was more than I wanted to handle.

A STEP FORWARD

I was sorry I had not been more up-front with Bill. Be honest with friends and family. Let them know what you need and what you don't need. Not everyone realizes that a terminally ill patient (and the caretaker) may find visitors exhausting.

Make a list of what people can do for you so you're able to suggest an alternative to a visit. Help family members understand that because everyone is losing the same individual doesn't mean everyone feels the same. The grief experience depends on the relationship. Especially, let others know that sometimes *not* showing up can be as loving a gesture as appearing on the scene.

What Do You Give a Dying Woman on Her Birthday?

When my mother had first phoned to say her cancer was back, she got right to the point. "Face it, Barbara. I'll be gone in two months."

Two months?

That brought us to October 24, Mom's birthday. Two years earlier on her birthday, Daddy had died. *She's going to die on her birthday,* I thought, trembling.

I pushed the thought aside, but I had the terrifying sense that my mother had set a time limit for herself. Like a canker sore you learn to live with, I watched the date draw inexorably closer. But despite two close calls, Mom was at home on her birthday, *still alive.*

And insistent that I color her hair.

"I don't want Margo tittering about my gray roots," she said. Margo, her best friend, planned to drive over from the coast for Mom's birthday. I'd ordered a cake. Gifts were piled on a table.

Mom wore her new pink bathrobe and matching slipper socks. Her hair, dark again, curled naturally around her face. I helped rouge her gaunt cheeks. "You look beautiful," I said, and she did, as if some extraordinary energy had filled her, dimpling her cheeks, bringing a twinkle to her eyes. She laughed as if it were any birthday.

We gathered around: her daughter and two sons, three of her grandsons, her two sisters, her best friend. We sang "Happy Birthday." She opened gifts.

It was such a happy occasion that I went to bed buoyed with a sudden hope. Maybe she *would* lick the cancer. Miracles happen.

The next morning, I woke to groans and cries. Mom's eyes were dazed with pain. The ambulance siren screamed as we rushed to the hospital.

But for one special day, she had transcended her pain. Maybe *that* was the miracle.

A STEP FORWARD

$\mathcal{B}$e grateful for every small, good moment with your dying parent. A shared chuckle at a television show. A drive through the neighborhood to see the daffodils in bloom. A moment of prayer together.

Think of the minutes and days as an impressionist's landscape—a pointillist painting where small drops of paint spattered on a canvas create a larger, more beautiful picture, but one that requires you to step back in order to gain perspective.

Departure

When my mother returned to the hospital the day after her birthday, nurses pumped in morphine. The drug held her pain at bay, but clouded her consciousness. I stayed each night with her, dozing in the recliner near her bed, listening to her heavy, labored breathing. A week passed. At sunrise on November 1—All Saints' Day on my mother's Catholic calendar—her breathing changed. It grew quiet. I stood, stretched, then moved to her bedside. The night nurse, a kind, dark-eyed woman, had pinned a pink ribbon rose to Mom's hospital gown. Her face looked white and cold, so I brightened it gently with lipstick. I reached for her hand. It felt like tissue paper in mine. *Do you feel my touch?* I wondered. *Do you know, in your drug-induced coma, that I am with you?*

It seemed to me that she was like a boat edging away from shore, drifting slowly, inevitably toward the horizon. Soon, I thought, the boat will disappear, and only the horizon, gray and empty, will remain. I spoke aloud. "Mom, your family loves you. And I love you." Her breath slowed, and then—had it stopped? I couldn't tell. I leaned forward. "Mom, have you left?" Her face was still. She looked peaceful.

She had gone.

A STEP FORWARD

*J*t's a great blessing to be with your parent at the very moment of the soul's release. Even if your loved one is in a coma, you can connect silently by speaking through your heart. In *Our Greatest Gift: A Meditation on Dying and Caring,* Father Henri Nouwen wrote, "People of faith, who believe that death is the transition from this life to life eternal, should see death as a friend." Be comforted in the knowledge that for your parent, too, the moment of death can feel as if a peaceful friend has come.

Déjà Vu

*E*xactly one year after my mother died, I experienced an odd déjà vu. By chance, it was my turn to sit with my dying mother-in-law, Cosette, a gentle, kind lady I had come to know well in the sixteen years of my second marriage. We'd been told she probably wouldn't survive the night.

Even after her son's divorce, Cosette remained friends with her first daughter-in-law. She could have ignored me, but she didn't. After Bill and I married, she wrote frequent, cheery notes. She sent me her paperback mysteries after she'd read them. She even knit me a Christmas stocking to match the one she had knit for Bill.

Now, as I sat in her room, I marveled at the similarity of hospitals—the same stainless steel, fake wood, white walls, and yellow tiles. The same soft beeping noises from mechanical monitors. The same mixture of odors—urine, antiseptics, and now, the peculiar sweet smell of dying.

Cosette was in a coma, but I wanted her to know she was not alone, so I stroked her forehead and spoke quietly, assuring her that she was loved.

Yet my feelings were very different from those I had experienced with my own mother. A mother-in-law, no matter how dear, is *not* your mother whose womb embraced you, whose very blood fed you, and whose genetic traits are imprinted on your face and character. Besides, Cosette had made it clear after her husband died that she welcomed death. So I felt no deep sorrow. I was simply thankful to be with her so she wasn't alone as she made her transition.

A STEP FORWARD

The depth of your feelings when a family member dies depends a lot on your relationship. Don't decide in advance what you "should" feel. Don't ignore your emotions either.

Take comfort in what I learned by being with three people—my father, my mother, and my mother-in-law—as they died. In all three instances, faces grew peaceful, labored breathing became quiet, and death itself was like a gentle hand. These experiences brought me a calm certainty that we need not fear the *moment* of death.

Alzheimer's!

Alzheimer's is a terrifying diagnosis. When Corrie learned her mother had it, she felt as if something dark and heavy had dropped into her body. She looked at her mother, who perched on the edge of her chair like a small bird, her head tilted, her eyes as bright blue as ever, but with something missing in their depths. Swallowing hard, Corrie made her decision. "I'll take Mom home with me," she said. She closed her mother's home in Knoxville, Tennessee, and moved her to Arlington, Virginia, where Corrie lived and worked. For thirteen months, with the help of a "Mom-sitter" and adult day care, Corrie was able to keep her half-time job as a pediatric nurse and care for her mother.

Hardest were the nights. Corrie never got a full night's sleep. She would hear her mother wandering around, going to the bathroom, rummaging in the kitchen. When Corrie tried to lead her back to bed, her mom would often push away from her, arms flailing, like a bird beating its wings against its cage. "It was as if she knew something was wrong," Corrie said.

Eventually Corrie had to place her mother in a nearby nursing home where, for eight more years, she visited her three or four times a week. "Even though Mom couldn't remember my name, I always felt she knew I was someone who loved her. And you know what? Some days I'd arrive feeling really low about Mom, but once I'd pushed her around in her wheelchair and we greeted people, I always felt better. It was a cheerful place."

Still, Corrie remembers what she heard at one of her Alzheimer's caregiver meetings. "Your grief starts long before your parent dies," said the speaker. "You're mourning the mother or father you once knew who no longer exists." As she told me this, Corrie's voice quavered and her eyes glistened. Her mother died last year. Corrie feels no lingering guilt. She knows she did everything a loving daughter could do. What surprises her is how much sadness is still left. "I miss Mom. Although—" a hesitation, another tear. "I guess the mom I really miss disappeared ten years ago."

A STEP FORWARD

*W*atching a loved one's mind deteriorate is one of life's greatest losses. "You lose your parent by inches," said one grieving adult child. Whether you are a hands-on caretaker or live far away, if your parent has Alzheimer's or dementia, check out a support group where you can share your pain—and yes, your anger—with others who understand.

Feeling the Grief:

"My Parent Has Died"

*Y*ou never really feel alone in the world until you stand on your parent's grave.

~Gary Small
Director of the Center on Aging,
UCLA

Shopping for Daddy

𝒯wo days after my father's death, I accompanied my mother on a shopping expedition unlike any other. We stood inside a room filled with coffins, each with a lid up, like rows of grand pianos. The funeral director said, tactfully, "I'll leave you two alone."

I pointed to a luminous white container with a baby-blue interior. "Now *there's* a casket."

Mom chortled. "Can't you picture your dad in *that*? He'd rise up and shout, 'Erna, get me out of here!'"

Slowly, we walked down the row of walnut caskets, oaken caskets, steel caskets. Each with a neat sign stating its price.

"Remember Marilyn Dewey?" said Mom. "Her kids put her in a rent-a-casket."

"*Rent*-a-casket?"

"She wanted to be cremated but have an open casket at the viewing. One that looked nice. After the funeral the body was transferred to a plain coffin for—you know, the oven."

"Huh. Rent-a-car. Rent-a-casket."

We giggled again.

Mom and I are like two preteens shopping for their first bras, I thought. *Covering our nervousness with jokes.* I remembered a famous Mary Tyler Moore show in which a television clown died, and Mary started giggling uncontrollably at his funeral. I was beginning to feel just as silly.

"Mom, look at this one!" An imposing sign announced, "Guaranteed moisture-proof for fifty years or your money back."

"Can't you see the next generation digging up Granddaddy to check out the guarantee?" This time we laughed so hard it brought the funeral director back. "Is everything all right?" "Fine. Just fine," I gasped.

Eventually, we chose a casket with a pearl-gray satin interior. When my father retired as an Air Force colonel, he had saved one uniform to be buried in. "The blue will look nice against the gray," said Mom.

Life is lived in the details, I thought, as we drove away from the funeral home, *and death is experienced that way, too.* In details, like selecting a casket. And finding something to laugh at while you're doing it.

A STEP FORWARD

𝒜ccept your moments of laughter as gifts. Laughter is permissible in mourning, just as expressions of joy for a life fully lived are valid at a funeral. Laughter offers temporary anesthesia from the terrible pain of grief. Be grateful for the gift.

Final Words

𝒥 glanced appreciatively around the nearly-filled chapel. Daddy would like the turnout, I thought. Our family milled about at the front, greeting neighbors and friends who came up to speak. My daughter glanced at my father in his casket. "It doesn't look like Granddaddy," she

whispered. "It doesn't look like *any* real person."
I agreed, even though I nodded when my mother said, "I think Cy looks very nice, don't you?
I'm glad we left his glasses on."

My mother's generation, more than mine, wanted open caskets (Her generation even took photos of the deceased). Though I might have preferred a closed casket, I saw how viewing the body confirmed death's reality for many people. In earlier times, Mom and I—and maybe my sister-in-law Eileen—would have washed and dressed the body, and in doing so, become intimate with the actuality of death. Now, I thought, the most a family member could do was gently touch a beloved face as it rested against a satin pillow.

No, I amended, there was something more. Family could eulogize. I had stayed up late the night before working on the remarks I planned to make. Like my brothers with theirs, the eulogy I'd written was my final gift for the father I revered and loved.

When it was my turn, I placed my notes nervously on the podium. Tears were close, but I swallowed hard and blinked them back. "Cy Lemmon had a great sense of humor," I began. "A week before his surgery, he told his grandsons that the rocks in the San Diego hills were *growing*. He said they'd grow faster if we played a little rock music." I saw smiles and heard soft laughter. *Good.* I wanted everyone to feel my dad's twinkly sense of humor, his ethical stance in life, the leadership qualities that brought innate respect, and the love he felt for his family. I wanted, with my words, to bring alive for a moment the man we had come to mourn.

A STEP FORWARD

*W*riting a eulogy is an extraordinary catharsis. Putting words on paper gets you in touch with your feelings and gives you a unique opportunity to pay tribute to someone you love. It helps you face death's reality, while at the same time, reminds you of your parent's well-lived life. If the moment of the funeral has passed, writing a eulogy can still be a cathartic exercise.

Go off by yourself with a pad of paper. To help your own emotional release, begin a page, "I'm so sad because. . . ." To start your eulogy, write the words "Here's what I remember best about. . . ." Think of your parent at different ages and in different roles—as spouse, employee, church-goer, hobbyist. An accountant friend said, "Usually I hate writing projects, but when I wrote about my mother, the words just *flowed*." Don't worry that you'll break down when you read aloud at the services. Most people are surprised at how well they do. If a sob breaks through, it only emphasizes how much you care. And you are, after all, among friends.

Mourning among friends is the function of a funeral. It provides a ritual, and it's through ritual that we proclaim life's transitions. A funeral celebrates, too. My church of origin, the Catholic church, now calls a funeral service the Mass of Resurrection and uses white vestments instead of black to signify eternal life. Your eulogy is one way you help celebrate your parent's life.

Men and the
Dead Fathers Society

At Daddy's funeral, my brother Jack was quiet. There was a pinched look to his face, and his eyes held shadows. He spoke very little as he shook hands with other mourners. His wife Eileen told me he retreated afterward to his workshop. Though Jack earned his living as a lawyer, woodworking was his passionate avocation, just as it had been for our dad. I could picture Jack in his workshop, the radio turned low to a classical music station, a backdrop to the now-and-then buzz of his jigsaw. The unheated air would be brisk but not cold. Jack would stand at his workbench, focused on the bowl he was making—the carefully selected woods to be planed, sanded, polished, and glued into intricate patterns.

My younger brother Rob was no carpenter, but he shared another of our father's passions—boating—and in the weeks after Daddy's funeral, Rob often launched his cabin cruiser into the gray quiet of the Seattle Sound. He went out alone, powering the boat across the waves, feeling the water thump against the hull, remembering the days he and his dad had boated together.

Writer Colin McEnroe calls it the *Dead Fathers Society*. "You see a sense of wounded surprise among men whose fathers have died," he wrote. "They are clobbered. They didn't know. They didn't expect the unspoken truths and unanswered questions that would sprout in the space where their fathers stood." It's not that daughters don't deeply mourn, but they express their grief differently.

A STEP FORWARD

$\mathcal{I}$f my father's body had been cremated, Jack might have followed the example of a man I read about who designed and constructed a wooden container for his father's ashes. The women in the family gathered in the house, but the men congregated in the workshop, and while the grieving son worked, the men told stories about the deceased. The workshop offered a meaningful activity and gave the men a safe place to feel their pain. They were able to laugh together. And cry.

How you mourn may be defined by your gender. Grief experts say men are more likely to keep their pain to themselves, go off alone to mourn, take physical and legal action, or become frenetically busy, filling every waking minute with some activity. Women will gather with others and sit with their grief, sharing verbal and physical touch. If you're a woman, do not expect your brother or your spouse to grieve exactly as you do. Acknowledge and honor the gender differences in how we process pain.

Forever Gone

The reality hit me a week after his funeral:
My father is dead.
I can never call him back. Never write to him or
talk to him again. Never hear his laughter—that rich,
rolling chuckle—or watch his eyes light up as he sees
me, or feel his strong, square hand on mine. Never
laugh at his silly jokes, or tap my foot as he plays his
harmonica or discuss world events or try to stump him
on a crossword puzzle.
He is gone.
The totality of death washed over me like a
tidal wave, swamping me in emotion.

I found myself saying aloud, "I miss you,
Daddy," and wondering, "Is your soul nearby?
Does your spirit exist somewhere? Is there an
essence of you still aware of me?"

I returned from California to my home in
Kansas City, and tried to go back to my usual
life. But it was fall, and as I drove down roads
where leaves fluttered into piles of orange and
rust, the barren trees reminded me of endings.
The car radio seemed to play nothing but minor-
chord music. Haunting, sad melodies.

I wondered if humans weren't like a bunch of
ants. You're born. You die. What a joke to try to
find some cosmic meaning to life. Did any of us
matter?

One night I got really angry at my dad. The
force of my rage startled me. I stomped around
my bedroom, raising my fist, tears streaking my
face, screaming out loud, "Why didn't you take
better care of yourself? Why didn't you get a

second opinion? Dammit, why did you let your-self die?"

I overheard my husband tell a friend, "Yes, Barbara is handling her grief very well." I wanted to scream, "No, I'm not! I'm sad. And angry."

A STEP FORWARD

*M*ourning is an up-and-down process, so it's natural to experience rage, depression, sadness, a sense of futility—the feelings can cycle through you in a single minute. Anger is a normal (though not inevitable) response to loss, and won't leave on its own. It burrows in and festers, growing larger and larger until you acknowl-edge it. There are healthy ways to discharge your anger and respond to overwhelming sad-ness. Get physical by punching a pillow. Scream (closed cars are good). Exercise vigorously. Vent into a tape recorder. Play back, then erase. Write a letter to your deceased. Then ritually burn it. Call a sympathetic friend. Let those close to you know how you are really feeling. Don't put on a happy face because you think it's expected. Grief denied is grief unhealed.

Closing the Family Home

I once sent my two brothers a heartfelt letter. "Promise me we'll never fight over our parents' 'stuff,'" I wrote. I had read a magazine article about family feuds and I didn't want it to ever happen to us. At the time, our parents seemed a long way from death and my brothers dutifully promised. After my mother died, I took a deep breath.

Now I would find out if the promise could be kept.

My brothers and I met on a windy Monday to close our parents' home and distribute their possessions. Rob brought packages of round, colored, sticky labels: red, blue, and yellow. We started in the living room, and agreed to take turns choosing "keepers." Once selected, the item would be slapped with a sticky label. My color was yellow. "To decide who goes first," intoned Jack, "we'll use a time-honored selection process called *rock, scissors, paper.*" All three of us laughed. Somehow, starting off with a child's game made things easier.

My parents had lived all over the world and their home reflected it: ivory statues from China, wood blocks from Japan, cut glass from Europe. I noticed each of us seemed naturally drawn to different things: Rob had the artistic eye. Jack was the sentimental one. I was more practical.

As we chose, we reminisced about our selections: the Chinese vase Jack had always liked, the German cookie-jar Rob remembered from his childhood; the silver coffee urn that had special meaning for me. We were taking apart the symbols of our parents' life together, yet I felt a poignant awareness of the intangibles we had received—the love, laughter, and solid values.

At day's end, we tackled my dad's color slides and sixty photo albums. Rob grinned. "I'm learning a lesson here. Always put people in your pictures because when you die, your relatives toss the scenery shots."

Oh, that made us laugh. I laughed so hard, tears sprang to my eyes, and as I wiped them away, Jack said, "I'm sure going to miss 'em," and we knew he didn't mean the pile of scenery slides.

A STEP FORWARD

Resolve to keep animosity out of the selection process when going through your parents' possessions. Remember the Gospel of Matthew which says "the important treasures are not those that moth and rust destroy . . . store up for yourselves treasures in heaven . . . for where your treasure is, there your heart will be also" (Mt 6:19).

If there are particular family mementos that you or your siblings feel affection for, and you can discuss them while your parents are alive, do so. Yet always keep in mind the bottom line—at the end of life, it will be your relationships that matter, not your material acquisitions.

Beyond Bricks

My parents had moved into their home just ten years before they died, so it held no childhood memories for us. My grandparents' house was a different matter. It was a large Victorian, filled with enough nooks and crannies to delight any child.

After my grandfather's funeral, which occurred three years after my grandmother died, my mother and I stood sadly on the sidewalk facing the house. My cheeks ached with unshed tears. We no longer had the right to walk inside. The house of her childhood—and in many ways, of mine—had been sold.

I grieved, along with my orphaned mother and her sisters and brothers because we had lost the family center. Years later, I listened as a man I knew blubbered, "It was only a house. Why am I crying like a little kid?" He couldn't understand his own feelings. "It was just a bunch of bricks," he said.

But of course, it wasn't just a bunch of bricks, any more than my grandparents' house was. Overlaying a home's stucco, wood, paint, carpet, tile, and bricks are the memories. The Christmas you crept downstairs before everyone else was up to see if Santa had come. The boisterous Sunday breakfasts after church when your dad made pancakes. The snug, safe feeling when it was storming outside, and your mother came to tuck in your covers. Even sad memories, like the day your dog died, are wrapped in the brick and stucco of your family home.

When you lose the family home, you lose a precious core. A sacred space. Your grief is natural and deserves expression.

A STEP FORWARD

Your family home may be gone, but your sense of family isn't. Years pile up quickly. Don't wait for someone else to plan a reunion. In some families, an eldest sibling creates a new "home base" where the family meets. Other families choose to meet in a neutral location—a resort, or even a cruise ship—rather than the memory-filled hometown. What matters is getting together. "Where thou art—that is—home," wrote Emily Dickinson. Sacred space is any space filled with love.

Amnesia

Kansas City sparkled with Christmas lights and tinkled with Salvation Army bells. In my client's office building, a huge tree decorated the lobby. I barely looked at it as I punched the elevator button. Upstairs, I sat down with the company president to discuss some advertising plans. As I reached into my briefcase, I gasped. "Oh no, I grabbed the wrong file." He looked irritated. I couldn't blame him. "I'm sorry," I stammered. "I don't know how this happened."

But I did know. I blinked my eyes, embarrassed by the rush of tears.

Should I say to him, "My mother just died"?

But wouldn't he say, "*Just?* I thought she died on the first of November. That was six weeks ago. You're not still grieving, are you?"

Maybe he wouldn't say it. But others had.

Everything seemed strange. Like a puzzle missing a few pieces. Or like a road shrouded in fog. I started crying in the middle of listening to one of my favorite Brahms symphonies. I kept forgetting things.

I asked the client if we could reschedule, and rode down again in the elevator. Sadness weighed on my shoulders with a physical heft.

A friend whose sister died of cancer, said

about her own grief. "It was like having early Alzheimer's. I would walk into a room and stand there, wondering why I came in. I'd pick up car keys. Put them down. Forget where I parked my car. I couldn't concentrate. I'd read three pages of a book and realize I didn't understand a single word I'd read." Another friend said she spent her first three days back at work in a fugue state, and later couldn't remember a single thing that had happened during those days.

But the best description came from a kind neighbor who said, simply, "You're experiencing the amnesia of grief."

A STEP FORWARD

The important thing to realize about mourning is that it's normal to feel slightly crazy. You will forget things. You will drive your car as if on auto pilot. You will stare at the papers on your desk and feel paralyzed to get any work done. This might be a good time to carry a small notebook with you. Write down things you need to remember. Don't rely on your memory. Let your boss know why you're not functioning at your usual one hundred percent. Be patient with yourself. Be as understanding of *you* during this time as you would like others to be.

Memories

Memories of my mother tangled in my mind like multi-colored strands of thread. So much reminded me of her. On an office elevator, I overheard two people discussing an upcoming trip to Nova Scotia. By the time they get off on the fifth floor, I was teary-eyed. Mom and I had talked about traveling to Nova Scotia.

At Christmas when no gifts appeared wrapped in recycled paper and ribbon, I laughed sadly, remembering Mom and her thrifty habits.

My heart quickened one day as I caught a glimpse of a woman striding across a parking lot with my mother's fast-paced, no-nonsense, shoulders-back walk. I even started to follow her, to call, "Mom, wait!" Then I remembered.

Yet I am grateful for my memories because I recall what my youngest son Andy said as he left for college. "Mom, I was so young when my daddy died, I can't quite remember him. I reach and reach and almost touch him, but not quite. I've always envied my sister because she was older and can remember. All I have are family stories."

It was the first time I realized that when you have no personal recollections, it's like a second loss. So now I rejoice in my colorful tangles.

*B*e grateful for your memories, even if they fill you with sadness now. "Remembered joys are never past," wrote poet James Montgomery. Eventually the pain does leave, and your memories will weave themselves into a tapestry where the happy and sad, the light and the dark, create a beautiful pattern.

Somebody's Child

"*I*'m not ready to be the family patriarch," said Tom. "In a lot of ways, I still feel like a kid myself." Tom was forty-five, but as he spoke, the rest of us—a support group of four—nodded our heads. All of us had lost parents in the past year, and none of us felt ready.

"There's no one ahead of me anymore," said Maura. Her voice rose, and she blinked rapidly, rubbing her eyes like a little kid instead of the accomplished professional that I knew her to be. "I don't want to be the oldest generation."

For all of us, it was our first real sense of our own mortality.

"Even if you live totally independent lives— even if you're a corporate CEO and never ask your parents for advice—there is, at some deep core, a sense of comfort in knowing you are still *someone's* child," explained our grief counselor.

If you're lucky, she said, your parents are the ones who cheer you on and always think you're wonderful. Even if they're not cheerleaders, they serve as a buffer zone. They stand between you and forced recognition of your own mortality. What she said made sense. The four of us had lost our buffers. No wonder we felt vulnerable and scared.

"I'm grieving for my parents," said Ginny, another group member, "but in an odd way, I'm grieving for myself. Because suddenly I realize that *I* am next. I don't like knowing that. Not at all!"

A picture flashed in my mind. I was standing at the edge of a steep cliff. The wind was blowing. I had nothing to hold onto. I was afraid it would blow me over.

A STEP FORWARD

Ѿhe vulnerability of realizing you are "next" happens inevitably. Gradually, you will feel more comfortable in your new role, especially if you look for ways to mentor those coming along behind—your children, your nieces and nephews, even, in some cases, your grandchildren.

It also helped me, after both my parents died, to "adopt" a parent figure. I began to communicate more often with my mother's two sisters, and on Mother's Day, sent cards to Aunt Helen and Aunt Jean. I made a point of visiting my Uncle John, who had my father's wry sense of humor. My friend Liz continues to visit the residents in the nursing home where her mother lived the last year of her life. "They're so happy to see me, and it gives me the feeling of staying connected to Mom," says Liz.

Expressing ourselves to others—both ahead and behind—makes the edge of the cliff seem less frightening.

Sorrow Doesn't End in Three Days

*W*hen I walked into a neighborhood bookstore, looking for a book on grief, the plump, sixtyish clerk pointed to a shelf of books. Then she said, "My mother was eighty-four when she died last year. No one understands why I'm still so sad. But," she continued, with a trembling mouth, "we lived together after Dad died, and she became my best friend." Tears fell. "I'm all alone now, and I miss her dreadfully."

I wasn't sure what to say, but as we continued to talk, I realized that she expressed what so many of us feel. Our sorrow isn't lessened because our parents have died at an "appropriate" age. Yet who understands that? After three days off from work, you're expected to move on. Your boss may express superficial condolences but look annoyed if she finds you inexplicably weeping at your desk. The friend you thought would understand and listen becomes impatient and says, "But your mother died three months ago. Don't you think it's unhealthy to keep dwelling on it?"

A STEP FORWARD

Grief counselors say it takes most people about two years to complete the mourning for their parents. And if your relationship was conflicted, or you had issues that were never resolved, grief work can take longer. You may even need some professional counseling. Our society doesn't support—and is even afraid of—the natural course of bereavement.

Give yourself permission to feel your sorrow, even if the world expects you to move right on. There are thousands of emotions associated with loss. They must be accurately perceived, endured, and finally mastered. If you don't find support from your immediate circle, investigate grief support groups sponsored by hospice, mental health facilities, or even funeral homes. Grief work needs to be shared with someone who doesn't show impatience, censure, or boredom. Another source of support is the internet. As more baby-boomers lose their parents, chat rooms are springing up where you can talk to others who have lost a parent. Support systems can help you process grief in a healthy way.

Loss Revisited

On February 19, four months after my dad's death, I sat at my desk, staring out my office window at a gray wintry day. A peculiar feeling began to course through my body, cold, like the flow of icy water down a mountain in the spring, splashing and overflowing into a sense of such profound sadness that I began to sob, great gulping sobs that made my shoulders shake and splashed tears on the paper in front of me. "Come back, come back," I yearned aloud, weeping for my mother, my father, and—oh my God—weeping for my first husband John, whose birthday it was, and who had died twenty-two years ago when his Navy jet crashed. I didn't understand it. Why was I weeping for John? Why did it suddenly feel as if he had died yesterday, and I was again a shattered young widow in my twenties? I clutched my arms around me, hugging myself, weeping for all the losses in my life, yet not understanding. I had long ago found closure in my grief over John. I had remarried. Life had moved on. Why was it coming back, that bleak, terrible sorrow? How could it hurt so—again?

A STEP FORWARD

ℬertha Simos wrote in *A Time to Grieve*, "A loss remains ever alive in the unconscious in which there is no sense of time. Past, present, and future coincide in our minds. Past losses are aroused when set off by a current loss, just as current losses evoke fear of future loss." It was natural, I realized, that as I faced the physical loss of my father, I might grieve again for my husband, whose too-early death had altered my world so profoundly. Once I understood that my feelings were normal, I felt better. Still sad, but no longer in a state of turmoil. Learn all you can about the *process* of bereavement so your emotions won't frighten you. Today, many resources are available.

Broken Heart

I loved pronouncing the name of my first husband's Italian mother. *Sarafina Rosina.* The syllables tripped off my tongue. They still do. Sara called me the miracle who replaced her daughter who died, a stillborn first child she had planned to name Barbara. I called Sara my "other mother."

I married Sara's oldest son John. In 1968, when he was killed while flying in the Vietnam War, his body was lost forever in the South China Sea. Sara, bereft of even the body of her son, was lost in the agony of grief. Six months later, she died too. Her doctors labeled it an aneurysm, but the family knew better. Sara died of a broken heart.

At her funeral, I felt oddly removed from the scene, as if I weren't really there, or as if I were participating in a play where I knew my lines, but felt no emotion. I loved Sara, I thought. *Why didn't I feel more?*

Fifteen years later, while driving down a highway in the Midwest, I heard a radio news report about a woman, twenty-five, who had drowned. Her body was not recovered. The young woman's mother was interviewed, and you could hear hysterical devastation in her voice.

My mind began fashioning its own scenario. It was my own daughter—now twenty-five—who died. As my imagination spun out details, tears began pouring down my cheeks. I started to sob. My grief was so intense and so astonishing that I pulled off the highway. I bent over the steering wheel, and wept—uncontrolled wails that petered out finally into hiccupy sobs.

When I looked up, the cornfield and the busy highway beside it seemed freshly colored, the way the world looks after a rain. I felt light-headed, but also, in a curious way, as if my heart had lightened.

A STEP FORWARD

A psychologist friend helped me understand. Now that I was the mother of an adult child, I was able to empathize with my mother-in-law's anguish when her son died, without even a body to make it real. The disembodied radio voice had triggered my unfinished grief over Sara and over my own sense of loss when John's body was not recovered.

If your parents' death prompts feelings that include sorrow for an earlier loss, seemingly unrelated, don't be frightened. Accept your feelings as a gift. Any grief you set aside will come again because grief must be processed. It's life's way of helping you find closure.

"Changing Roles:
Comforting My Parent
Left Behind"

To see your parent so vulnerable is hard. At the same time, you feel sorry for yourself. It's like having two sets of children instead of one.

~James Atlas
writing in *The New Yorker*

Unspoken Words

In November, my mother said, her tone wistful and ruminating, "It doesn't seem as if it's been just thirty-two days since Cy died. It does seem like a long time since last summer, though." Her eyes held a faraway look, as if she were not seeing me, but rather the backward passage of those summer days. "Your father felt bum all summer. His heart and his hip bothered him. Made him cranky. It was so hot at night, and he slept so restlessly, that I finally began sleeping in the guest room. We weren't communicating much, to be honest. But I never dreamed that after surgery, he would never be able to talk to me again. So many things were left unsaid."

Such a poignant remark. I ached for my mother, and for all spouses who are left with the feeling that "a lot of things were left unsaid." I wanted to hold and comfort her, but when I reached out, she pulled away. I thought she must be afraid. If she allowed herself to be held, she might give in to all the anguish she felt, and my mother was never one to expose her deepest feelings. Instead, she drew back, and made her voice brisk. "Well, no point dwelling on it. I've got to decide what to do now that Cy is gone."

A STEP FORWARD

It's important to realize that you can't change your parents' characters or their way of handling life's transitions. If your surviving parent wants to talk about the emotions that follow a spouse's death, make yourself available to listen. But if the preferred way of handling emotions is to act practical and get busy, honor that response, too.

Fixing Things

After Daddy died, Mom frequently phoned me, usually at night, her voice often brittle with anger. "I need your brother's help," she fumed one night. "There's a hole in the kitchen window screen. Your father would have fixed it in a jiff. But Jack says he's too busy right now. Why won't he come?" Her voice was querulous and irritable.

"Mom, Jack *is* busy." I tried to speak gently but she didn't hear, until finally, to get her attention, I snapped in a voice as angry as hers. "Dammit, Mom, can't you ever listen?"

The phone grew silent. My hands felt clammy on the receiver. I was ashamed that I had yelled. "Mom, Jack is a lawyer with a busy practice and two half-grown sons who are playing team sports. It's all he can do to get to their games. Why don't you call a handyman service? You can afford it."

"I don't want some stranger over here. I want my son."

No, I thought, *you want your husband.*

Daddy was a putterer. A fix-it guy. He could always be depended on to glue together the pieces of a broken china plate, or to hang a shelf just where she wanted it, or to fix the wiring in a malfunctioning toaster. For forty-six years, she had counted on him to fix what was broken. But no one could mend what was broken now.

It wasn't the hole in the screen that needed fixing, it was the hole that had come into my mother's life, dark, yawning, immense. The space that my father had filled. She wanted my brother to fix it, but he couldn't, nor could I.

Helpless, I tried to think of something to say. No words came.

A STEP FORWARD

A psychiatrist friend told me, "Even if you and both your brothers moved in with your mother, it would not be enough. You could not fill her emptiness or ease her pain. Everyone has to do their own grief work." What I *could* do for my mother was to be there to listen. And that's what you can do, too. Whatever form the grief takes, don't judge and don't offer quick solutions. Just listen.

Moving On

My mom was a sociable person who liked to go places. She and Daddy had traveled most of the world on one junket after another. At home, she could host a dinner party with an hour's notice. But when she became widowed, Mom discovered what other newly single women learn: she was no longer part of the "couples' crowd." And many of her single women friends didn't like to go out at night.

"A bunch of Nervous Nellies," said my mother with disdain. They wouldn't drive into L. A. with her to see a play or go farther than a few blocks away for dinner at a restaurant. "They want to be home with their doors locked by 7 p.m."

Forced into a stay-at-home existence at night, Mom wandered through a house that seemed unnaturally silent, even with the TV on. Though she switched on the lights, there were shadows in the corners she had never noticed when my Dad was alive.

Some of her friends told her they liked living alone. "I loved Harry, but finally, I can eat beets again. Harry never liked beets. And I can read in bed at night. Harry always liked the lights out. Just wait awhile," said one widowed friend. "There's a lot to enjoy when you live on your own."

Not for Mom. She wanted her old life back. Left on her own, my sociable mother seemed to shrink. Her mouth took on a slightly bitter skew. I suggested she look into Elderhostel travel. Or take an art course. "You always said you'd like to paint," I prodded. But Mom seemed unable to move on.

A STEP FORWARD

Mourning has its own timetable, unique to each individual. If a year passes and your widowed parent is finding it difficult to handle a day's ordinary tasks, it may be time to ask, "Could my mother (or my dad) be experiencing depression?" Depression is a physical illness that can be triggered by an emotional crisis, and the depressed patient can be helped by medication. But don't be too quick to tell your widowed parent that it's time to move on. As columnist Ellen Goodman eloquently wrote, "There may be one-minute managers, but there are no one-minute mourners."

Girlfriends

(O)ne of Mom's special griefs after Daddy died was the loss of their planned reunion trip to Weisbaden, Germany, where they had lived on an Air Force assignment twenty-five years earlier. They had looked forward so eagerly to their trip! I was sad, too. Now it would never happen.

But shortly before the first anniversary of my father's death, Mom's travel agent sent her information about a packaged European tour. "Will you go with me?" Mom asked. "I'll pay for both of us."

From the anxious note in her voice, I could tell how important it was that I go. Instinctively I knew she would not make the trip on her own. Yet I was nervous, not only because it meant taking three weeks off from work. It also meant spending three weeks in the company of my mother—and that scared me. We hadn't spent three weeks together since I was twenty years old, and in recent years, we frequently clashed. What if we started arguing? What if we bored each other? What if. . . ?

Our first stop on the two-week tour was Paris. On our second night there, our guide took us to a nightclub. It was a club designed for tourists, and the entertainment was only so-so. But during the show, I heard my mother laugh. A girlish giggle, rising to an amused chuckle, then exploding in a rollicking guffaw until I was infected too, and in minutes we were both shrieking and holding our sides. At that moment, I wasn't sitting next to my bereaved mother. I was sitting beside a woman who was having fun. *This is the woman my father fell in love with*, I thought.

For the rest of the trip, we were like girlfriends. It wasn't until our plane touched down in L.A. that my mother confessed how scared she had been to spend three weeks with me. "But we had a good time, didn't we?" she said.

I gave her a hug. "Yes, we did."

A STEP FORWARD

*I*s there a trip that you and your parent might take? Even if it's just a day trip, look for a way to put yourselves into a different environment and see how it helps to abate the anguish. Changing locale is not a permanent solution, but it's an easement, an opportunity to briefly vacation from the heaviness of sorrow.

New Love

"*I*t wasn't that I thought my father would never marry," said my friend Marge, "but to get engaged six months after Mom died? I can't believe it! And I'm angry!" Marge's father is an attractive man in his early seventies, with a thick head of white hair and a golf-course tan. He and his wife had been high school sweethearts, and they'd been married nearly fifty years when she died of cancer. "How could he forget Mom so fast?" cried Marge.

But he hadn't forgotten her. "I loved Sally deeply," he told me in a private conversation. "Ours was a *good* marriage. I didn't expect to meet someone so soon, but I went to one of those support groups for older single people and Marie—she's divorced—she and I went out later for pie and coffee and . . . well, we hit it off." His voice grew a trifle testy. "The kids are the ones who encouraged me to go to the support group." He sighed. "Sally was sick for a long time before she died and I did a lot of my grieving then. Now I want to share my life with someone. Is that wrong?"

I thought about my widowed father-in-law. He had married the widow of an old friend. They'd run into each other at the cemetery while visiting their spouses' graves.

It's natural to want to share your life.

I patted the hand of Marge's father. "You're not choosing Marie over Sally. Love expands. Give your children time to realize that."

A STEP FORWARD

When thinking about helping a widowed parent, most adult children don't think about how they'll respond to their parent's recoupling. Of course there are practical considerations—some careful estate planning might be one—but the greatest tribute to a marriage is surely a willingness to commit again. An anonymous poet wrote in the Middle Ages, "The well of life is love, and he who dwelleth not in love is dead." If your widowed parent finds another love, get to know the person. Act as if you are glad your parent is no longer alone, and you may find yourself feeling that way sooner than you expected.

"I Can Do It Myself!"

Jean is an older friend of mine who moved to the Montana mountains after she and her husband George retired. They were in their mid-seventies but still actively hiking and skiing when George died in a freak ski accident. Jean was devastated, but not only by the loss of her husband of forty years. "My kids are trying to take over my life," she told me on the phone six weeks after the funeral. Her daughter and son were convinced she should move out of the mountains and take up residence near them. "You should be near your grandchildren," insisted her daughter.

"My grandkids are teenagers," retorted Jean. "They don't want me messing up their daily lives. They'd rather come visit me now and then in my ski condo."

"But you can't live alone out there," said her son. "It's too dangerous."

"Piffle," said Jean (her favorite swear word). "The mountains are safer than your interstate traffic."

Her children were not convinced.

Don't try to rearrange your surviving parent's life. Allow your parent to grieve, and talk about the deceased. Be there—in person or by phone— and available to listen with encouraging, sensitive comfort. Make offers. "May I help you with your income taxes?" "Can I interest you in joining us on a family vacation?" But don't insist. Your widowed parent is a grownup. Give some credit for decades of intelligent living.

"Dad Should Never Have Left!"

"I didn't expect to feel this way," said Scott. His voice held a note of puzzled surprise. A tall, handsome guy close to fifty, Scott was in my grief support group. For the past twenty years, he said, he'd had a cordial, golfing-buddies relationship with his dad. Plus, he appreciated the financial generosity his dad had shown Scott's children. But it was a different matter when Scott was fifteen. That's when his father left his mother for another woman, and for ten angry years, Scott and his sister refused all their father's overtures.

A few months ago, Scott's mother died. What startled Scott was how *enraged* he became—all over again—at his dad for leaving his mother. "Dad called to say he was sorry about Mom's passing, and I yelled at him on the phone. This— this fury poured out! By the time I threw down the receiver, I was shaking. I felt like I was going to throw up. My wife was staring at me, her mouth open."

Scott found himself remembering things he hadn't thought about in years. The pain he'd felt—as if someone had hit him really hard in the gut—when his mother told them his dad had left. The tears that kept rolling down his mother's cheeks, puddling against her neck. She didn't sob, didn't even seem to know she was crying; the tears just fell and fell. His own anxiety when he came home from school and, day after day after day, found his mother still lying in bed, her hair uncombed, staring at the wall, acting as if she didn't hear when Scott and his sister urged, "Mom, get up. Come on, Mom."

Scott's voice was tight. "Dad didn't think about us. Just himself. And now Mom's dead, and he's out there in Arizona playing golf in the sunshine with that blankety-blank woman he married. . . ." Losing his mother had spun Scott right back to the painful year when their family collapsed.

A STEP FORWARD

$\mathcal{N}$ew losses reopen old wounds. Sometimes the issue is not how to *comfort* your surviving parent, but how to deal with your own conflicted feelings for that parent. Scott mourned for more than his mother. Though he had gradually rebuilt a relationship with his dad, it had stayed superficial. They were "golfing buddies." Issues from the desertion had not been faced. With the grief group's encouragement, Scott sought some short-term, one-on-one counseling to help him work through his unresolved issues surrounding his parents' divorce. Then he flew to Arizona and confronted his dad. They talked, and his dad was able to express regret at the hurt he had caused his children. Eventually, Scott built a better relationship with his surviving parent. But it took time. If Scott's story awakens emotions in you, remember that anger and grief ignored do not go away. They go underground. Short-term counseling could be a useful step.

Sometimes a Relief

Tina's father died three years after his first heart attack, and although she was sad, she admitted, "It was almost a relief because I knew it was coming and for three years, every time the phone rang, I thought it might be *the* call. When it finally happened, it put an end to the agony of waiting." She had some mixed feelings. She felt angry because her father had diabetes as well as heart disease, and had never taken care of his health. Yet she took comfort in knowing he had died quickly, and at work, just as he always said he hoped he would.

"I had a dream that my father died and came back," said Tina. "I asked him, 'Are you well?' In my dream, I didn't want him back unless he was well. I felt guilty when I woke up, but that's how I felt."

What surprised her were the feelings that rose nearly eight months later. She found herself thinking, "Well, Dad, you've been dead long enough. *Now* you can come back." That's when the awareness of death's *foreverness* began to sink in. That's when she felt the totality of her loss.

A STEP FORWARD

You, too, may find relatively quick closure after your parent's death. It doesn't mean you loved your parent any less. Grief counselors have learned that when a relationship was a good one, a sense of closure will come earlier than in a conflicted relationship. Be grateful for the peace you feel. Look for ways to acknowledge your parent's role in your life: perhaps by hanging photos or continuing a family tradition that was important to your dad or mother or by staying in touch with close friends of your parent.

Is God Unfair?

It is hard enough to watch a loved parent die from an extended illness. But there is certain logic to illness. A virus has entered the body. A genetic flaw has kicked in. Painful—but understandable. How do you understand when a drunk driver robs you of your loved ones?

Gerald Sittser and his family were returning from a weekend trip when a drunk driver stuck their minivan head on. He lost his mother, his wife of twenty years, and a four-year-old daughter (he and his other three children survived). In his book, *A Grace Disguised*, he wrote, "One of the worst aspects of my experience of loss was this sense of sheer randomness. The event was completely outside my control. An answer to the "why?" question eluded me. Maybe, I thought, there really is no God and no meaning to life."

Dr. Sittser, a professor of religion, grieved deeply. For several years, he wished he could change the events of the fateful day that took his loved ones. He resented and railed against the awful reality thrust upon him. Gradually though, he came to a different place.

"Loss has little to do with fairness," he wrote. "On a superficial level, living in a perfectly fair world appeals to me. But deeper reflection makes me wonder. In a fair world, I might never experience tragedy, but neither would I experience grace." For grace is always an undeserved gift.

Dr. Sittser decided he could live in a universe where people do not always get what they deserve, either positive or negative, as long as it's a universe which contains grace and compassionate mercy along with painful loss.

A STEP FORWARD

If you have recently lost a parent (or any loved one) in a random accident, you may read Dr. Sittser's words and want to throw this book against the wall. The awful relentless pain is so strong that even someone of great faith must weep and cry, "Why?" Don't expect that you can do more than you are ready for, but pray—even if you pray into the darkness—for God's transforming grace that one day you will be able to say, as Dr. Sittser said, "Out of my pain, God became a living reality to me as never before."

A Golf Ball for Dad

Josie stood at the open casket of her Irish-politician, golf-loving dad. "I'll miss you," she whispered. And with a little smile, knowing how much her father, seventy-three, would appreciate the gesture, she dropped a golf ball into his casket. As she told me this story, I smiled too. Josie had inherited her father's sense of humor, and she had given him just the right send-off.

It was different when her mother died three years later of a massive heart attack at the age of seventy. As Josie looked at her mother's body, she was struck by an overwhelming awareness: *I came out of your body. I grew inside you. You were joyfully pregnant with me. I was your baby. And now you are gone.*

Suddenly, "I felt so empty inside and so vulnerable," said Josie, without a trace of a smile. "I didn't want to think about both my parents being gone. I threw myself into wife-ing and mothering my own family because it was the only way I knew to reclaim my lost roots, my sense of permanence."

She didn't visit her parents' graves, or even think about them a lot, at least not consciously. But after a time, she began waking from sleep, her face curiously wet with tears. She knew she'd been dreaming about her parents.

One day, Josie pulled out boxes of family photos to make a scrapbook for her sister's birthday. "I found a photo of my dad as a darling young man and then this wonderful photo of my mom—they were both in their prime before any of life's problems had touched them. I took the photos to a photo shop to make copies, and suddenly, right there in the shop, I started bawling. I couldn't stop."

Josie realized she had grief work to do and she began paying attention to her sadness. Today, she still dreams about her parents. But now she is less likely to wake up weeping, and more likely to wake up with a smile. "My dreams comfort me," she said. "I think that means my mourning is ending."

A STEP FORWARD

$\mathcal{B}$aby boomers are creative in their personal send-offs to deceased loved ones. Josie dropped in a golf ball. Another friend's grandchildren put hand-made gifts in their grandmother's coffin. Ask yourself if there is anything special you would like to do for your parent. What public or private ritual will help you in your mourning process?

Josie also experienced her mother's and her father's deaths very differently. Your mourning, too, may contrast because your relationship with each parent was different. There is no "right" or "wrong" way to mourn as long as you do it. Don't use frantic busyness as a way to deny your feelings. Josie's dreams brought her back to the task at hand. Over and over, I heard from experts, "To complete your grief requires you to go through it, not around it."

It Should Never Have Happened!

Beverly's mom was an energetic, red-haired real estate agent who looked younger than her sixty-one years. Bev liked to brag that she and her mother were best friends, and a lot of her same-age friends said they envied the two their relationship. When her mom went in for orthoscopic knee surgery, Bev expected her to come home the same day.

"I went with Dad to pick her up and while we waited outside the recovery room, we talked about what a terrific woman Mom was," said Bev. "Suddenly, I saw a bunch of doctors and nurses run down the hall. You could feel panic in the way they ran, and I don't know why, but instantly, I was scared. Dad told me I was silly, it couldn't have anything to do with Mom—she was just having knee surgery. But about twenty minutes later, Mom's doctor came into the waiting room. His face was white, and he kept swallowing. I remember noticing the way his Adam's apple bobbed up and down. He still wore his surgical greens and he stuttered a little when he said, 'I—I'm so sorry.'" An embolism, totally unexpected, had gone straight to her heart.

"I heard the doctor speaking, but it was like he was far, far away. Like I was floating somewhere and I said, my voice very definite, 'You're wrong. Mom's not dead. It's not her time to go. She needs to get me through the teenage years with my daughter. I can't do it without Mom.'

"Then I felt my dad's arm around me, and I heard someone crying, but it wasn't me, it was my father. And I kept saying stupid things, like, 'Dad, don't cry. It can't be Mom. It's not her time.'"

But it was. She was gone.

A year later, Bev still feels lost without her.

"Sometimes I simply stand and scream, 'How can this be? It was simple knee surgery, for God's sake!'"

A STEP FORWARD

There is no answer to the inexplicable. A seemingly healthy woman dies after outpatient surgery. Who can explain it? No one. "When there is no answer to *why*," said one grief counselor, "you need to ask *how*? And *what*? What can I do to find comfort? How can I find strength to go on?"

Bev learned everything she could about her mother's death to satisfy herself that there was no medical malpractice. She joined a *Tai-bo* class, because it helped work off her anger. She started to garden, a hobby her mother loved. She talked to her dad a lot, and by comforting him, found it helped her. For six weeks, she met weekly with a grief counselor. And she prayed, especially words from the ancient psalms, "My soul is in anguish . . . turn, O Lord, and deliver me."

You can't escape your pain, or, in some circumstances, your anger. But you can experience healthy mourning by answering the questions, *how* and *what*.

"How Could You, Dad?"

*J*ulie's eyes looked haunted as she spoke to me. "How *could* he?" she cried. "How could he leave us like this, angry and hurt and—and—" her hands fluttered helplessly in the air. "How could he?"

Suicide is one of the most difficult deaths to handle because it leaves survivors feeling fear, rage, guilt, depression, and the always aching question, "Why?" Survivors cry aloud, "I should have noticed he felt depressed." Or, "Why didn't she talk to someone?" Or, Julie's poignant question, "How *could* he?"

Julie's father took early retirement from a job he loved. "Forced retirement," he called it. Marriage problems were exacerbated once he was home all the time. He became depressed. Started drinking. Julie, who lived several states away, didn't know about the accumulating problems.

"I loved my father," she cried, "but now I am *so* angry at him. We were always close. Why didn't he confide in me?" She took a deep breath. "He was the one who said, 'No problem is so terrible that you can't deal with it in the morning.' It was one of his favorite expressions. Every time I'd get mopey as a teenager—you know—figure my life was over because some boy didn't ask me out—there would be my dad, throwing his arm around me, pushing his glasses up on his nose, and saying that stupid, stupid cheerful—" she swallowed, stopped, and her shoulders heaved. Tears rolled down her cheeks, "Oh, Dad, how could you?" she whispered.

A STEP FORWARD

At one time, suicides were denied a church burial. Even now, when mental health professionals explain that clinical depression can hamper a person's ability to think rationally, family members may feel too shamed or guilty to talk openly to one another about their pain, leaving individuals to struggle by themselves with unresolved grief.

Don't try to do this alone. Some deaths cry out for survivors to seek professional help or talk to others who have walked in their shoes. Grief counselor Helen Fitzgerald says adamantly, "It takes more than one person or one event to cause a person to take his or her life. You did *not* cause the suicide." There is a lot of literature on suicide. Learn as much as you can so you can believe what Fitzgerald said. Consider writing a letter to your loved one, expressing your anger about the unanswered questions and also affirming your love. Realize that your pain will take longer to heal. Be patient with yourself. Ask for God's grace to assist you. Believe that even this will ease (for it will). You may never forget, but one day you will accept, and you may even forgive.

Finding Closure

My friend Dottie displays such exuberance for living that it's easy to believe she is her father's daughter. He was a charismatic Armenian immigrant who came to this country unable to read, write, or speak English. Yet he built a dry-cleaning business that became the third largest in America.

For three months after his cancer was pronounced terminal, Dottie flew halfway across the country every other weekend to be at her father's bedside. They spoke by phone every day. "We talked in great detail about his life, and I told him repeatedly how wonderful he was and what a great father he'd been," said Dottie, her voice softening in memory. She was with him, holding his hand, when, ". . . he pulled his hand away and I knew he was ready to go."

Today, several years later, Dottie says, "I never felt my father left me. It's as if he's alive—just not in his body. I call on him when I need help and I talk to him regularly."

A STEP FORWARD

Dottie is one of the lucky ones. Her father died knowing she loved him. They had communicated openly and well. She had a comforting sense of closure. If you and your parent parted as Dottie did from her father, rejoice, even in the midst of your sorrow, because eventually, you will find that your parent is still wonderfully present in your memories and will be there for you. If yours was a different kind of parting, and you are feeling conflicted, remember that no one today has to heal alone. Funeral homes, hospitals, community mental health centers, and churches offer support groups.

"He Wouldn't Stop Smoking!"

Ted's father smoked two packs a day for forty years, and eventually carried an oxygen tank the way some people carry a briefcase. A tube glided through his nostrils like a narrow green snake—and still he smoked.

Ted didn't see his father much after his parents divorced. For a long time, he felt as if his dad had abandoned him, but when he was in his mid-twenties, Ted's company transferred him to the city where his father lived, and Ted and his dad reconciled. Less than a year later, Ted's dad lost a lung to cancer.

Ted had smoked, too, all through high school and college, but he quit when his wife got pregnant because neither one wanted to expose their children to second-hand smoke. When Ted caught his father lighting up after surgery, he was furious.

"How can you keep smoking? You're killing yourself! You'll deprive my children of a grandfather!"

His dad's eyes were red-rimmed. His hand shook. "I want to quit. . . ."

"Then do it. *I* quit!"

But his father couldn't. Or wouldn't. The cancer spread. A year later, he died.

When Ted talked to me about his grief, there was so much rage in his voice that I urged him to seek counseling so he could find some closure, some peace. His emotions were all tangled. He loved his father, felt abandoned by him, felt he'd found him again, and now had lost him forever.

"I quit for my child!" raged Ted. "Why couldn't my dad quit for me?"

A STEP FORWARD

Ted's anger obviously involved more than his dad's smoking. Conflicted grief is the very hardest to handle. Are you angry as well as sad? Are there unresolved issues with your parent? It's very common. You need a listener who can allow you to express your hostile feelings without retaliating or arguing, so you can find out what's *behind* them. Anger usually masks yearning, shame, fear, or hurt. It's important to deal with the accurate emotion. To help you, some counselors encourage finger painting or drawing pictures with the non-dominant hand (that is, the hand you don't write with), and then writing a description of whatever your drawing tells you. Other counselors encourage clients to talk to an empty chair as if it held your deceased. Tell the "person in the chair" what you're feeling. Give yourself permission to feel your anger because if it's not expressed, it may go inward and emerge as depression or physical illness.

From Death to Birth

We were airplane seat-mates—strangers to each other—which is probably why Richard spoke so candidly. He was a tall, handsome architect in his early forties.

"As a kid," said Richard, "I was afraid to go home after school. Both my parents were alcoholic. They abused each other and me. My mother's tantrums went on and on until my father would scream, 'Shut up!' I was an only child, so I responded the way only children often do in alcoholic environments. I tried to be the extra-good little boy. As a teenager, I dutifully went on weekend trips with my parents in their motor home, even though it forced me to listen to more of their tirades. I was afraid to 'disappoint' or break away from them.

"Finally, after college, I married, and did move away. But not far enough. My mother's letters often contained hurtful comments. Sometimes, it would be days before I could bring myself to read them. My wife dreaded them as well."

Richard felt tormented and demeaned by his parents, and after his father, and then his mother died, he slid from grief into a serious clinical depression.

"My wife left me and I lost my job. It took a lot of counseling before I began to understand my parents and myself. Eventually, I realized that my mother had suffered from chronic depression as well as alcoholism. This knowledge didn't ease the pain that I'd experienced growing up, but it helped me understand and forgive her."

As our plane bumped to a landing, Richard admitted that his grief encompassed so much anger that it was a long time before he had straightened it all out. Slowly, though, his life got on keel. He remarried. Recharged his career. Fifteen years after being orphaned, said Richard, "I'm a pretty happy man. Ironically, the death of my parents, which pushed me into counseling, helped me give birth to my self."

A STEP FORWARD

Not every one has an idyllic parent-child relationship. Your parents (and mine) were fallible human beings, constricted by their own upbringing and their own parent tapes. This is one of the reasons it helps to learn family history. If you discover (as one woman did) that your grandmother was orphaned at birth and taken in by an abusive aunt and uncle, it may help you understand her weaknesses in parenting your mother, which, in turn, affected you. We reach the final stage of "growing up" when we surrender our need to want our parents to be perfect.

Like Richard, you may discover that your parents' deaths open the door to a better understanding of your family dynamics. Don't feel guilty if your life feels freer or if orphaning becomes a springboard for you to pursue a set-aside dream. Life calls on everyone to become all we have in us to be.

Too Young to Say Good-Bye

Jim's father died at the very start of a new year. Even today, twenty years later, Jim shakes his head as if he can't quite grasp the reality of it. His parents had attended his sister's New Year's Eve open house, but left early. As his father walked into his living room, he muttered, "I don't feel so good," and before taking another five steps, collapsed of a massive heart attack.

His dad was sixty-three. Jim was thirty-three. "I'd been away for several years in the military and then college," said Jim. "When a job brought me back to my hometown, I was finally at an age when Pop and I could start relating as adults. We'd have lunch once a week. He was a supervisor at work so I'd pick his brain about work issues. He liked that. And he had a great sense of humor—something I had never appreciated as a teenager. We were just getting to know each other. And then—boom—he was gone."

No one told Jim that he was too young to lose his father. In fact, Jim doesn't remember anyone saying anything in particular. "My brother and sister were several years older, and went on with their own lives. My wife never talked about it. We had the funeral, I went back to work, and that was that. Pop was just—gone."

Jim missed having an older, wiser man to confide in about job problems and career moves. He felt adrift, unsure of himself. In hindsight, he looks at difficulties that cropped up at work after his dad died, culminating in a job loss, and thinks they were tied in, somehow, with a lot of unresolved grief.

"It's funny how you can miss someone, even twenty years after they're gone," said Jim. "I've never stopped wishing that Pop and I had had more time together." Now that his son Jeff is a young adult, Jim is trying to spend more time with him because, "Well, you never know."

A STEP FORWARD

*W*here are you and your siblings in your family's birth order? If you have a younger sib who's had less time to know your parent from an adult perspective, be alert to ways you might step in as a "caring, older friend." And if you need comforting, don't wait for someone to offer. Let your spouse or a good friend or an older brother know that you need to talk about your grief. Look for a mentor. As Jim discovered, grief unresolved can show up in other arenas. Like Jim, you might want to consciously reach out to your young adult children. Help them know you as a person as well as a parent. Never think, "We'll have time for that later." As Jim discovered, you never know.

Words Unsaid

"*I*t's not always your natural parent you grieve," said Colleen, a tall, slim woman I met at a women's conference. Colleen wore a well-cut suit, and her blonde hair was pulled into an attractive French twist. As we sipped coffee, she told me, "I had a rough childhood. My parents were divorced and both were pretty self-absorbed. By my teen years, I was living in L.A. with my mother and running wild—smoking, doing drugs, cutting school, shoplifting. I was headed in a bad direction and decided to go live with my father and his second wife. I wanted to "clean up my act," but my father mostly ignored me, so I began acting even wilder.

"But Dad's wife Marcia spent time with me. She listened. Sometimes I felt she was pretty tough, but she had more belief in me than either of my parents. She convinced me I could turn my life around. Thanks to her, I turned out okay.

"After I finished school and left home, my dad and Marcia divorced. A few years later, my dad died, and I lost touch with Marcia. Recently, though, I started thinking about her. Maybe because I'm planning to get married soon, I wanted her to know what an amazing, long-lasting impact she had on my life.

"But I was too late. She died in a car crash two years ago. I'm so sorry I never let her know how important she was to me."

A STEP FORWARD

*J*f there is anyone in your life who needs to hear you say, "I love you," call that person *today.* If it is too late to say the words in this life, write a letter. Pour out your feelings, then hold a ceremony. Light a candle, letting the flame symbolize the love in your heart. Touch the candle to your letter and drop your letter in the fireplace. As the smoke curls and the paper turns to ashes, prayerfully release your love. Relationships don't cease when someone dies; they merely become different.

No History

"No one is left who remembers my childhood," said Cicely. Usually she spoke as a self-assured bank manager, but now voice dropped to a whisper. She was an only child. Her grandparents had died years ago, and each of her parents was an only child which meant Cicely had no cousins.

"People with siblings are lucky," she told me, "because then there are others who remember the Christmas you were five and got your new sled. Or the summer you vacationed at the cabin on the lake. Or Roger, the tom cat you dressed up in baby clothes. I have no one who can answer if I say, 'Remember when?'"

Her touching statement caught me off guard. I had never considered what it must be like to be the only one left in your family. I thought about the family jokes and stories my brothers and I still share. Silly reminiscences that have no meaning for anyone else.

To be alone with your own history—"That's a lonely place to be," I agreed.

A STEP FORWARD

If you're an orphaned only child, you may want to "adopt" a sibling. I know two women friends who sent each other "official" adoption papers.

Stay in touch with your parents' oldest friends, the ones who always greeted you with, "Look how you've grown! Seems like only yesterday you were a baby." They know your history— part of it, anyway—and they may tell you stories about your parents that you've never heard.

Share your childhood history. If you're a parent, tell your children the stories of your childhood. My kids loved the "Sally" stories I told them when they were snuggled in sleeping bags in our camping tent. My "Sally" stories were actually stories of my own childhood. Spend time creating scrapbooks that tell your story.

Develop a network of friends you can count on, and tend your network as you would tend your garden. Offer *your* home or apartment as a holiday meeting place for other orphans (or those who simply have nowhere to go). Build your connections so you won't feel alone.

Her Dilemma

Sheryl admits she has a peculiar dilemma. Her mother quipped, before she died, that she wanted to be cremated and put in an urn on her daughter's mantel, so she wouldn't miss anything. And that's where she is, inside an urn on the mantel, with her picture next to it.

After her mother died, Sheryl forged a deep bond with her dad. She called him every day. "He became my best friend," she said. In 1998, her dad moved in with Sheryl and her family because of worsening kidney disease. On Valentine's Day,

Sheryl's husband drove her dad as usual to his dialysis treatment. When they returned, her father said he was tired and just wanted to sit in the truck for a while. Sheryl thought he was sleeping. Later she went out to check. "Come on, Daddy, wake up." When he didn't stir, she felt a burst of panic and started to cry. "Daddy, you have to wake up!" By the time paramedics arrived, Sheryl was crying hysterically. Her father died soon afterward.

Sheryl's father also wanted to be cremated, but hadn't said where to place his ashes. And he had no favorite spot in nature, like the ocean or the mountains. "I didn't want two urns on the mantel," said Sheryl, so temporarily, while she tried to decide between the two, her dad's ashes went into a black plastic box in a drawer.

Even as she mourned her parents, especially the dad who became her best friend, Sheryl also found a certain humor in her "peculiar dilemma."

A STEP FORWARD

J, too, chuckled at Sheryl's story. Her laughter is another reminder that even in sadness, humor can lurk, and that's what life is—a balance of sorrow and joy, tears and laughter. We cannot appreciate one without the other.

Her dilemma is also a reminder that it's a good idea to ask your parents, while they're alive, if they have any special requests after death.

The Road Is Long and Winding

Carol blinked back tears. In the other bedroom, her ten-month-old daughter cried. But here, in this room, her mother lay dying. How could it be? Mom was only fifty-three. Her mother whispered, "We all die eventually. What counts is life eternal." She paused, coughed, then said, "I'm glad you came home."

The baby's cry became a yowl, and Carol, grateful for the distraction, hurried to pick up her daughter from the crib. Carol was twenty. Against her parents' wishes, she had eloped with her high school sweetheart. When she got pregnant, her husband left her, and she'd come home, ready to admit her mistake, and longing for the comforting arms of her mother. Instead, she learned her mother was dying of cancer. *I'm losing everyone*, she thought. And she couldn't take time to mourn. She had her small daughter to take care of, along with her grief-stricken father.

This all happened twenty years ago. Last fall, on her fortieth birthday, Carol entered counseling, looking for help to finally mourn her mother. She realized she had raised her daughter "in a hurry," as she put it, trying to cram everything into Kelly before she turned eighteen, because, after all, that was all the time Carol had had with her mother. But Kelly thought her mother was overly-strict and she rebelled. They're still repairing the rift in their relationship.

"I grew up quickly after mom died," mused Carol. "I couldn't lean on my dad, because he was too numbed with his own grief, so I took responsibility for myself and my daughter. Mom's early death taught me not to hold grudges, because who knows how long your life will be? But I put my own sorrow on the back burner, and that created problems in other areas of my life."

A STEP FORWARD

*Y*ou don't always have the luxury of focusing on one traumatic event in life. Events may dictate what must be handled first, forcing you to put your grief for your deceased parent on hold. But grief put off doesn't disappear. Weeks, months, or years later, it demands to be witnessed. That's when you may find yourself falling apart.

Don't be frightened if that happens. Don't feel guilty, either, if you put your grief behind the immediate need to get a job or complete a divorce or handle a problem child. Think about it this way—your parent would understand. If you're a person of faith, trust that you'll find the grace to work through your sorrow when the time is appropriate. Just as Carol is doing.

"Not Who I Thought He Was"

"*I*'m resentful that Dad didn't plan better. He left a mess, frankly. It's robbed me of my respect for him." Alan, thirty-six, is the executor of his father's estate. But the estate has nothing in it but unpaid bills and bulging files that tell Alan more than he wants to know about his father's addictions, failures, and as Alan put it, "general screw-ups." Such as the insurance policy whose beneficiary his dad forgot to change. In the hospital, before he died of cancer, he managed to whisper that he wanted his elderly mother and his two grown children to share the insurance benefits, but it was too late. The policy named his father's second wife—a woman he'd divorced six years earlier—and she chose to keep the money.

"I feel angry and disappointed," said Alan, "because I'm the one who lives nearby so I was the one who had to close up his house and go through his papers. And I've been forced to learn that my dad was never who I thought he was. You know the real irony? I could have straightened out his financial affairs. It's what I do for a living. Why didn't he call on me?"

He released a long sigh. "You couldn't find a nicer guy than my dad in terms of hanging out together. We went canoeing three weeks before he died and had a good time. But now—" he shook his head. "At least this mess helps me better understand why my mother divorced him, but—" another mournful sigh. "I didn't want to know what I've had to learn about my dad."

A STEP FORWARD

It's painful to discover, too late to talk about it, that your parent had feet of clay or led a secret life, or left a financial mess for you to clean up. How do you follow the commandment to honor a parent who has lost your respect? That's when forgiveness becomes necessary—not only for your deceased parent, but for yourself. First, acknowledge what Alan called "the screw ups." Feel your anger. It's a natural response. But for your own well-being, so your soul doesn't shrivel into bitterness, be ready to start the forgiveness process. Because it is a process, it won't happen all at once. It can take years. But if you are committed, you'll find the grace to achieve it, and that will bring freedom to you. A good place to start is by reading aloud Psalm 23, substituting "we" for "I." Picture your parent saying the words with you.

"I Want My Mommy"

"I could only say this here, not to anyone I know," wrote Ed in his chat room posting. Ed described himself as thirty-eight, single, six-foot-two, with the body of a weightlifter. He held a graduate degree and was known in his company as a hard-charging, tough manager. "I know it sounds stupid to say this, but I feel like a little kid again. It's like I see myself as this little boy, lost in a crowded store, calling for my mommy. I can't believe she's gone."

Ed and his mom, a divorced business woman, had become good friends as adults. They both lived in California and liked to ski and hike.

"A couple of years ago we even took a trip together to South America. We had a great time. I called Mom my cheap shrink. I could call her and know she would just *listen*. She didn't give advice. Or judge. I worked out my own answers by talking out loud to her. "When the docs found cancer, she went so *fast*. A couple of months was all. I miss her so much. I could never say it out loud, but inside me, there's this little kid crying, *I want my mommy*."

Ed got a lot of responses. One man wrote, "Wow. You capture the way I feel. I'm embarrassed, too. I'm a married father of three. I have responsibilities. My mom and I weren't even such great friends. She was just—my mom. I never thought about her not being there. When my youngest boy hollered for his mommy the other day, I almost broke into tears. I wanted my mommy, too."

A STEP FORWARD

How sad that grown men feel it's a shameful secret to admit they miss their "mommies." Psychologists say that everyone has a small child inside, and in certain situations, no matter how adult your responses are most of the time, your vulnerable "inner child" will cry for mommy. When a mother dies, it's a primal loss. Early childhood fears of abandonment are often re-experienced. If you feel like a lost and lonely child, don't be ashamed to seek comfort. One of the best ways is to let someone hold you. A friend of mine wrapped her arms around a neighbor who had recently lost his mother, and simply rocked him. Remember, you're not alone in yearning for your mommy.

Old Rivalries

$\mathcal{M}$arlaine is an attorney I occasionally have lunch with. When I told her about writing this book, she said, "Watch out for old family fights to flair." Marlaine and her younger brother Tom were always at loggerheads when they were kids, she explained. Marlaine felt her mother babied Tom and took his side at her expense. "One Saturday, both of us kids were in the kitchen and Mom came in and asked if Tom wanted a sandwich. Tom said 'Sure,' so Mom made him one. When I said, 'Hey, Mom, how about me?' you know what she did? She handed me the bread and peanut butter to make my own." Marlaine still sounded incensed.

As adults, Marlaine and her brother went in different directions and her brother's work took him out of the country. They hadn't seen each other in three years when Marlaine's mother died of a heart attack last spring. When they reunited, the childhood tapes replayed.

After the funeral, Marlaine said she would like to keep her mother's engagement ring. Tom went through the roof. "You and Mom never did anything but fight! I should have her ring. I was the one who really cared about her."

"Are you insinuating I didn't?" cried Marlaine. Their voices rose. She turned to her father, waiting for him to take her side, but he just looked stunned. "Your mother is dead and you two are fighting over a ring? You disgust me."

Marlaine broke into tears and fled the room. When Tom departed for the airport that afternoon, the two of them still weren't speaking.

Six weeks later, feeling calmer, Marlaine went to see her father. She told her dad to go ahead and send Tom the engagement ring. "Dad gave me the rest of Mom's jewelry. And that's where it stands." Marlaine took a bite of cucumber sandwich. "But are Tom and I friends? I don't think so."

A STEP FORWARD

*D*id you fight a lot with your brother or sister when you were kids? If siblings haven't worked through childhood animosities, rivalries may flair when a parent dies, and adult brothers and sisters usually fall into the same family roles they held as children. What psychologists call "infantile feelings of deprivation" may also be reactivated. At a subconscious level you want proof of your parent's love, and a particular object symbolizes the proof for you.

Since fights over things are often generated by unresolved feelings toward parents, stay alert. If squabbles begin, it's a warning that fragile emotions are involved. Defer your decisions for a few weeks. Let emotions cool. Borrow a tip from the brothers who used the french-fry method of dispersal, named after the way their mother divided plates of french-fries when they were kids. One brother divided; the other chose. Consider what underlying reasons might be causing your sibling's insistence on a particular object. If you've been successful at separating from your parent and developing a good, adult relationship, think about the intangible gifts you received, then take the lead in refusing to let *things* get in the way of long-term family unity.

Feels Like Yesterday

Delia sent me this e-mail: "It's been five years since my father died and two years since my mother passed on and I miss them both like it was yesterday. I was only thirty-five when I watched my father go from being a strong-willed, independent man to an almost childlike state after his illness. I had to carry him to the bathroom and take care of all his most personal needs. The dad I had relied on for advice and comfort was not there anymore.

"It was like rubbing salt into my wound when my mom died three years later in her sleep. Mom couldn't bear the weight of being alive without my dad. Even her grandchildren could not keep her going.

"It seemed so strange to become an orphan. No longer someone's child. Even though I'm married, I felt as if I lost my safety net. I'd always known that if I ever got into serious trouble, my parents would be there for me. Now—there is no one."

Delia expressed what so many people have said to me, mournful statements in different voices:

"Dad and I were the family's comedy team. We made everyone laugh. Who's going to be my straight man now?"

"My mother and I were in the same career field: advertising. We bounced ideas off each other. Passed on job information. She was my professional mentor. The cancer took her so fast, I never got to prepare. I keep looking for her and can't believe she's not here."

"They were my cheerleaders. They gave me bragging rights. No one else lets you brag about yourself like your parents."

"I lost a piece of my youth when my parents died. The family isn't whole anymore. I may never go back to my hometown."

A STEP FORWARD

When you share your experiences with others, it helps you realize you're not alone. While that knowledge won't lesson your sadness, it does remind you that your feelings are normal. Your mourning is natural. It is fitting to feel your grief. Fitting to mourn for as long as it takes. For some that will be a few months; for others, it may take a few years.

It's also good to know that one day your grief will pass. You can integrate into yourself the qualities in your parents that warm your heart. And let go of the rest. As other orphans have learned, no one completely loses their parents. In a unique and wonderful way, they become part of you.

"He who is remembered is not dead."

Finding New Meanings:

"I Complete My Grief"

*D*eath changes us, the living. In the presence of death, we become more aware of life . . . it can inspire us to decide what really matters in life—and then to seek it.

~Candy Lightner
in *Giving Sorrow Words*

Acceptance

Sometimes I say, always with a smile, "My mother and I relate better since she died than we did in the last few years of her life." Whoever is listening usually laughs or raises an eyebrow. But I mean what I say. Growing up Catholic, I often heard about the "communion of saints." To me, that meant I could ask a deceased holy person to be my intercessor with God, since, according to Christian teachings, the soul doesn't die. Saints, like angels, could be other-world guides and mentors.

If I could talk to a deceased saint, why not to my deceased parents? So after they died, I conversed regularly with my mom and dad. I liked to believe that Mom had found, in the passing of her earthly body, a wisdom that allowed her to happily embrace my life in ways she never had when she was alive. I felt she had reclaimed the good humor that an undiagnosed depression hid in her later years. I knew I no longer had to struggle to please her.

"Mom, I love you," I murmured one Sunday as the priest intoned prayers for the dead at Mass. "But Mom, I gotta be honest. You had a wicked tongue."

I could almost hear her say, "You're right."

Later, though, I spoke through my heart. "Mom, I understand you better now—how life's wounds affected you and sometimes made you say or do something that I found hurtful. And I remember all the loving ways you mothered me. Some of them I'd forgotten. Thank you."

I believe she appreciates that.

<u>A STEP FORWARD</u>

$\mathcal{J}$f you always wished your mom or dad saw you more clearly or accepted more of your choices in life, rejoice. Believe that the soul finds clarity beyond this life. Believe that the spirit of your parents is within you, seeing clearly who you are, accepting you, and loving you as God loves you. Unconditionally. Try loving your deceased parents that way, too.

Saying Thanks

$\mathcal{W}$hen I was twenty, I wrote a poem for my father on Father's Day, in which I compared him to a rock:

From its strong solidity,
there is a buoyancy.
Like a spring
I catapult and soar,
And yet return to rest.

I found the poem in my father's papers after he died. Frankly, I had forgotten all about it, but I was touched that Daddy kept it. I remembered something my friend Marianne said. Her father died when she was twenty-eight. "I wasn't through *needing* him yet," she said.

When I wrote my poem, I still needed my father. No wonder I described him as a rock from which I could take flight and soar. He encouraged me to try new things, and I believed he would be there if I needed to rest or get a second wind.

I ran my fingers across my girlish writing. How young my handwriting looked, each letter precisely rounded. I'd been catapulting and soaring on my own for years. But wasn't that because, at one time, my father seemed like such a trustworthy rock? I whispered words that went beyond need. "I love you, Daddy. Thank you."

A STEP FORWARD

How did your parent offer you the opportunity to catapult and soar? Even if your relationship held conflict, did that very conflict push you, like a young eagle, out of the nest? Think about it now. And say thank you.

Free to Be Me

Many orphaned adults told me they were surprised to discover that after their grief passed, they felt a new freedom to be themselves. Death acted as a springboard, freeing them from parental expectations or the need to cover up a lifestyle because they were afraid their parents wouldn't approve.

One woman said she felt freer to marry the man she loved, because, as she explained, "My folks preferred buttoned-up lawyer-types, and Loren was a laid back guy who wanted to open a surfing shop in Costa Rica."

A man in my neighborhood lived all his life in the shadow of his highly successful father. When Gordon became orphaned, he used his inheritance to start a company in a field totally different from his father's. Gordon found midlife success in computers.

One of the more dramatic changes occurred when a city-bred husband and wife, both of whom had lost their parents, left their comfortable Midwest suburb and moved into a trailer in the Colorado mountains. "Our children were grown and self-supporting," explained the husband. "Neither one of us had living parents to take care of. We were free to reinvent our lives. So we did."

It is one of life's paradoxes that when parents die, it sometimes clears the stage.

A STEP FORWARD

Counselor Maura Conry asks clients to review their lives and write down all the ways they have conformed to or rebelled against their parents' expectations. (Either way, she says you ignored the question, "What do *I* want?") Once your parents are gone, ask yourself which of their expectations or values are truly yours. Choose what to keep and what to discard. Now decide for yourself how you want to live the rest of your life. Then *live it!*

Unexpected Comfort

My college-age son Andy was six feet tall and built like a linebacker; in other words, built like my father. To Andy, whose own father died when he was four, Granddaddy was a beloved father figure. When he came to his grandfather's funeral, Andy fell into my arms like a little kid, sobbing as if his heart would break. I held him, and my tears mingled with his. I wept for my own loss and for Andy's double loss—his daddy and now his granddaddy when he was twenty.

Andy's voice was muffled against my shoulder. "I like to think Daddy was waiting for Granddaddy. And that when I die, they'll both be waiting for me." He paused, gulped, and added, "Death must be an explosion of knowing, don't you think? Suddenly all the pieces fall into place and the person who dies is swept up into a wholeness, a oneness with the universe. Does that make sense, Mom?"

What deep thoughts to emanate from someone whose daily life still revolved around reading college texts, playing rock music, and "checking out chicks." I hugged him. "It makes perfect sense."

I wondered what touch of grace produced his insightful words, "An explosion of knowing." The phrase comforted me. I was comforted, too, as I pictured Andy, long years hence, reaching beyond death to the place where his father and grandfather lovingly waited.

A STEP FORWARD

Sometimes comfort reaches us in unexpected ways, from surprising sources. I found it in the words of my son. My friend Lois, whose mother died unexpectedly, gained comfort from holding her infant granddaughter. "I saw that my mother's genes had passed through me to my daughter and through my daughter to *her* daughter, and that Life didn't stop, but went on, like a golden chain. It helped me feel I had not completely lost Mom." Keep yourself open to sources of comfort that may surprise you.

The Little Light

My second husband Bill stood at the podium in the unadorned chapel. The group was small— a dozen family members, clustered at the front. We had gathered for a memorial service prior to sprinkling the ashes of Bill's mother.

Slowly, Bill lifted a small votive candle. Ceremoniously, he lit it. The flame flickered, seemed about to go out, then steadied. He smiled. "This flame symbolizes my mother," he said. "She was just a little light, always in the shadow of her husband, my father. But in her own way, she shed a luminous glow."

He continued to speak, evoking a picture of his sweet, unassuming mother, using small homey details. He mentioned her pimento cheese spread which he loved as a boy. Now he bought it ready-made at the supermarket, but the taste still reminded him of her. He wore the green ski sweater she had knit for him in high school, though it was, he confessed, "a trifle snug." He remembered their bets over certain football games, "She was a real Packers fan," he said.

At the end of his remarks, he reminded the group that in her later years, his mother loved mystery novels. "She always appreciated a good ending," he said. With that, he bent over the candle, smiled, and gently blew it out.

A STEP FORWARD

It was very cathartic for Bill to compose and deliver the eulogy for his mother. I experienced something similar when I delivered eulogies for my parents. If you choose, the words you speak could be your final gift and a way to bring alive your parent's spirit to others.

When we returned home from sprinkling Cosette's ashes, Bill set the votive light on our coffee table, and often, in the evening, would light it. He usually smiled and said something like, "Glad to have you with us, Mom."

A physical symbol can help you keep the spirit of your parents alive—and alight. What symbol do you choose?

Many Mothers

After his mother died, David discovered a letter she had written years earlier. It was addressed to "All my children," with instructions to be read when she died. On the day of her burial, David and his brothers and sisters tore the seal and read the words written in his mother's familiar hand:

Later, I, too read her words. The ones that particularly stood out for me were these: *"Look around you for the mothers who remain: Mother*

Church, Mother Earth." Yes, I thought. And
Mother Nature.

Such a beautiful reminder! The connection
we feel to our mothers is so strong because all of
us at one time were physically connected in the
womb, gaining our nourishment directly from
our mother. But we still have other mothers.
I thought about the nourishment I received
from my "other mothers." Nurturing food for
my soul from Mother Church. A connection
through Mother Nature that tied me to all
humans, animals, plants, birds, fish, insects. We
inhabit together our beautiful blue spaceship—
Mother Earth.

I felt a sharp, sweet awareness: *I am not alone.*
I am one cell in All-Being. And I have many mothers
to nurture me.

A STEP FORWARD

*J*f you visit your parent's grave, look around
and reflect on the beauty of the natural cycle,
which returns the body to earth, "dust to dust,
ashes to ashes." At night, look skyward and
appreciate the stars that glitter in our universe
and your connection to it, as a being on Mother
Earth. If church is part of your life, realize the
nurturing it gives you. And if your spiritual journey is outside a church, touch a tree, feel the
breeze, lift your arms, open yourself in medita-
tive prayer to the beauty of All-in-All. You are
not bereft. Nor am I. We have many mothers.

Seeing the Gift

$\mathcal{A}$ few years before her death, I made a scrapbook for my mother. Well, part of a scrapbook. I wrote an essay about my grandparents' Victorian home and how much it had meant to me, pasted it in a scrapbook, along with a photo of the house, leaving the rest of the pages blank for my mother to fill in. I wrapped the book for Christmas.

In our family, Mom was known as the world's best gift giver. Name something in June, and Mom remembered it in December. But it was hard to give *her* a gift. Her usual response was, "I told you not to spend money on me."

That's why I was so excited about the scrapbook. Here was something unique and meaningful; a gift of no great monetary value but one I was sure she would treasure. It was a real labor of love, too, because I was unusually busy at work that fall.

When I called my parents on Christmas morning, I waited for Mom to ooohh and ahhhh over my gift, but she said nothing. Finally, I asked, "Mom how did you like the scrapbook?"

"It's very nice," she said.

Nice? Was that all she could say? My happy expectation trickled out like air from a pricked balloon. I was hurt.

A few months later, I visited my parents. Prominently displayed in the living room, I saw my scrapbook. Only now it bulged with photos and mementos. In a moment, I understood. Mom never found it easy to communicate her deepest feelings. She was *showing* me how much the book meant to her, the only way she knew how—by filling its pages.

When she died, I inherited the scrapbook. It's very precious to me now because I saw how precious it was to her.

A STEP FORWARD

*D*id your mom or dad's actions speak louder than their words? Maybe your parent was like my mom, unable to come right out and say "I love you," or dance a jig when you did something special. It's hard work, having to figure out how someone feels by observing their subtle "I love you" messages. But pick through your memories. If you look for ways your parent *showed* "I love you," you'll find them. And if you wish your parent had been more demonstrative, just remember: accepting our parents for who they were is the final step in growing up.

A Few of My Favorite Things

I have never been a collector of *things* as some people are. I've always said I'd rather collect experiences. But after my parents died, something peculiar happened. Certain *things* became very significant. I mentioned the scrapbook. My mother also left behind my grandmother's engagement ring, a very small diamond in an old-fashioned setting. Whenever I wore it, it was as if my grandmother's spirit somehow connected to me.

My parents treasured an antique grandfather clock, and when I had lived at home, its melodious chimes in the middle of the night always seemed to signify, "All is well." Now the clock is in my home, and I carefully wind it each day. Its chimes are like the voices of my parents, reminding me, "All is well."

There's also a silly item I kept. Something that would have no value to anyone else. It's the paper parasol that came in a cocktail my mother ordered when we visited a Paris nightclub. She saved it, and somehow, that makes it important to me.

A STEP FORWARD

One way to keep your parents alive in your heart is to treasure the objects that were significant to them, or that bring back your own happy childhood memories. Don't pack the object away. Display it. Hang it on the wall. Explain its significance to your children. *Things* as symbols go far beyond extrinsic value. An object that symbolizes is a memory-minder; a treasure that keeps your parents close to you.

Traditions

"If Mom gives you socks for Christmas, she'll wrap each sock separately so you'll have *two* packages, not just one to open." Everyone in our family knew it was so. It was part of our family legend. And when we poked at gifts under the tree, wondering aloud, "What is it?" my dad always chuckled and said the same thing: "A little red do-nothing with a string tied on it."

Just a year ago, while spending Christmas with my daughter Allison and her family, I saw one of her sons shake a package under the tree. "What is it?" he wondered. In a cheery echo of her grandfather, my daughter replied, "A little red do-nothing with a string tied on it." And on Christmas morning, she smiled as her husband unwrapped his gifts from me. "Mom, you're just like your mother," she said. "You gave Kevin golf balls and wrapped each golf ball separately."

So we pass along, from one generation to the next, our family rituals, stories, familiar sayings, special customs—all the traditions that recall our loved ones for us. Whenever I hear the words "a little red do-nothing" I see my dad, eyes twinkling, hands on his hips, wearing the outrageously patterned golf pants he liked, standing in front of the family Christmas tree. The image brings a smile and a spurt of happiness.

And when my grandsons grow up and start families, and their children poke packages under the tree, I have a feeling they'll say to their kids, "What is it? Why, it's a little red do-nothing. . . ." And in those words, my dad will live on.

A STEP FORWARD

*C*herished traditions create a sense of continuum. Yet different people, even in the same family, mourn differently. While you might want to maintain a tradition, your sibling might choose to let it go. Both of you are doing it for the same reason—because you miss your parents.

You may even find, as some people have, that the death of parents signals a freedom from traditions that have become burdensome. Several adult children admitted they felt a quiet relief at being able to dispense with fatiguing holiday travel.

Choose the traditions you want to continue. Let them be an ongoing reminder of your parents. And be understanding if your siblings make other choices.

Menus and Memories

These days, I usually cook healthy, simple-to-fix meals. But a while back, I pulled out a dusty, almost-forgotten, three-ring binder whose red-checkered cover was titled "My Recipes." Inside I found a hodge-podge of grease-stained note cards, recipes clipped from magazines, and a few inked-in binder pages, everything thrown in haphazardly.

I spied a note card in my mother's slanted handwriting. "Excellent make-ahead dish," she had written. I rubbed my fingers gently across her writing. *The casserole queen,* our family called her affectionately. Memories washed over me, fragrant and sweet. I was startled at the power of a cookbook to spark such vivid recollections.

But why not? Food is central in life. People gather together to break bread. We create traditions around meals. *Menus and memories,* I thought. It occurred to me then that I'd stumbled onto a very special way to create a family heirloom. Something as special and long-lasting as family genealogy, patterned quilts, or scrapbooks. Why not put together a book of favorite recipes and attach to each recipe the memory that went along with it? I would start with my mother's make-ahead dish.

A STEP FORWARD

In the months—and years—that lie beyond your parents' deaths, you will find unique ways to perpetuate their memories. Twenty years after his father died, Jim's sister gave him their father's pipe-stand. It had sat in her attic all those years, forgotten. As Jim refinishes it, he feels a renewed sense of kinship with his father. Such encounters with deceased parents—Jim's pipe-stand; my recipe card—are wonderful bits of serendipity. Surprise gifts. You can't make such encounters happen, but you can be open to them.

"Kiss Your Spot"

Whenever I say good-bye to my oldest grandson Jake, I turn his head—just so—and say, "Time to kiss your spot." Then I plant a noisy kiss on his neck a half-inch below his right ear. "I'll still be kissing your spot when you're twenty-two, Jake."

Jake grins. Without saying a word, I know he agrees, and that this normally "cool" kid who wouldn't be caught dead letting just anyone kiss him, is happy to let his Grammy plant one on. It's as if his "kiss spot" is a secret signal between us. What Jake doesn't know is that every time I kiss his "spot," I feel a happy flash of my mother's spirit. I recall another little kid—my son Andy—obediently turning *his* head so his grandmother ("Mom 2," the kids called her) could kiss his spot.

Andy and my mother had a special connection. He loved the way she made him real mashed potatoes, when I, a working mother, merely added water to a mix. He liked her willingness to listen, and he even liked her high expectations for him, because somehow she conveyed a rock-solid belief that *of course* he could meet them. When she died, Andy was twenty-two and had grown into six feet of sinewy muscle, but he still turned his head obediently so his grandmother could kiss his spot.

Now that I'm experiencing the special joy of grandparenting, I have a profound appreciation for the loving way my mother lived her grandparent role. When I take Jake on an "adventure," or we play a killer game of Scrabble or I kiss his spot, I feel as if I'm continuing something begun by my mother, and that through our responses to grandchildren, we are still connected, even beyond her death.

A STEP FORWARD

You, too, will experience a sense of continuum with your deceased parents. It will be unique to your own life: perhaps you become motivated to pursue a cause that mattered to them, or you'll see in yourself certain skills that your father or mother modeled. Maybe you'll be drawn back to a religious faith or feel inspired to pass on to your children's children the kind of love your parents offered your children. The greatest homage is a desire to imitate, so when you catch yourself acting like your parent, feel blessed. It's a reminder of connections that are not severed by death.

Rejected!

"When my friends talk about missing their mothers, I sit quietly and don't say a word," said Ronda. She was orphaned a decade ago, but hers is a different kind of pain. The last words Ronda heard from her mother were angry and rejecting.

"Since her death, I've tried to say, 'Mom, I forgive you—I know you had a series of minor strokes. Maybe they impacted your mind. I know you were displeased that I 'brought a divorce into the family.' I know I look like Dad's mother, a woman you never liked But after all, I was your child! Why couldn't you love me more?" Her voice cracked.

Ronda's mother died four years after her father. What convinced Ronda that she wasn't imagining her mother's rejection was her mother's will. Specific bequests were left to Ronda's sister and her sister's children. Ronda and her three children were cut out.

Such pain lingers in the soul.

"You learn to live with it," said Ronda, putting on a more cheerful face. "My mother's behavior made me think carefully about what I would leave my children. I don't want them to feel slighted the way I did, so I wrote a Will that cleanly divides whatever I have into thirds. I'll give my children any family mementos they want before I die."

More than *things*, however, Ronda decided to give her children what she didn't receive from her own mother—loving acceptance. She shows pride in their successes, compassion in their stumbles, and allows them to make their own choices, whether or not she agrees with them. I watched her at a holiday dinner with her daughter and two sons and saw the joy in her small grandchildren's faces as they cuddled up to their Nana, and I felt awed by her ability to give what she had not received. It seemed as if I saw the power of grace at work.

A STEP FORWARD

In some parent-child relationships, the great pain at death is the realization that a better relationship can never be achieved in this life. If your loss is coupled with such pain, you experience a double grief. In *Necessary Losses*, Judith Viorst wrote "Perhaps the only choice we have is to choose what to do with our dead. To die when they die. To live crippled. Or to forge, out of pain and memory, new adaptations." Feel your pain. And vow to live past it.

Final Closure

It is never too late to say farewell to a parent. Twenty-four years after Air Force Colonel Jay Morrison was shot down over North Vietnam and declared "Missing in Action," photos taken by the North Vietnamese were hand-delivered to Jay's wife Peggy and her now-grown children, Jed and Cindy. For all those years, they had never known for sure if their father was dead or alive. Now, fearfully, unsure of what they would see, Jed and Cindy looked at the black and white photos. They showed a pilot, face up, sprawled full-length on the ground, one arm flung behind his head. He'd been shot.

Cindy's chin trembled. "He looks asleep," she said.

"He was younger than I am now," murmured Jed.

For Jed and Cindy, the photos brought stark realization of all they had lost. "You were such a good mom," Cindy told her mother, tears coursing down her cheeks, "that I just accepted I didn't have a dad. Now it's like my nerve ends are raw and tingling. But it's good to feel the pain—to know what I lost. It will help me embrace other people in pain. I couldn't do that before. I'd think, 'So what's the big deal?' That's because I hadn't felt my own sorrow."

Although they will never know where Jay's body was buried, Jay's children found a peace that was denied to them for years. "It's like closing a book," said Cindy. "The grandkids no longer have to say, 'Grandpa Jay who's missing.' Now they can say, 'Grandpa Jay in heaven.'"

A STEP FORWARD

Cindy and Jed's experience of finding closure is one every adult child must seek, for until that important closure takes place, you cannot lovingly release your parents and move on with your life. The Morrisons' experience reinforces the timelessness of grief. Whether it's twenty-four hours or twenty-four years after your loss, you have to do your grief-work.

Because Cindy hadn't acknowledged her own pain, she couldn't empathize with others. As a minister's wife, this had been troubling. Feeling your pain allows you to understand the pain of others—and leads finally to a place of joy again.

Celebration of Birth

In order to please her mother, Ipeleng Kgositsile, an African-American actress, said she grew up wearing "masks" that hid who she really was. "I learned to deal with the world in the same way I dealt with my mother. I hid my emotions, my feelings, from myself."

After her mother died, Ipeleng wrote, "Our parting was God's way of allowing me to develop fully. I no longer lived in denial. Why pretend that I was never angry at my mother or that I never defied her wishes? My life—that time with my mother—is over and will be now and forever just a memory. By accepting this reality, I have finally put my mother to rest. I can feel her peace. My mother's death paved the way for my birth. I am blooming and that is a cause of celebration. Until we meet again, it is the greatest gift I could ever give her.

Reading Ipeleng's words reminded me how I, too, in an effort to please my parents, had worn masks that hid a lot of my core identity—even from myself. It's not that the proper middle-class mask I wore was wrong, it was simply not *all* of me. After my parents died, I felt freer to acknowledge my adventurous, free-flowing self—the part of me that would ride a motorcycle or pitch a tent in the Southwest desert or wear a Gypsy skirt and dance the night away. Like Ipeleng, I let my parents' deaths give me freedom to bloom.

A STEP FORWARD

It's appropriate to see in our parents' deaths an opportunity to give birth to more of our own true essence. There is no need to feel guilty. You're not demeaning your parent's memory by choosing values or behaviors that are uniquely yours.

Grateful

"*When* you're sixty-four and your parents are in their eighties and your mother has been help-less from a stroke for four years, your first emo-tion when she dies is simple relief," said Morgan. Morgan himself is seventy now, though he looks younger. "My mother was a bright, charming lady who always acted with great pro-priety. Her whole sense of self was affected when she couldn't talk, feed herself, or walk, so I was glad her ordeal was over. But once my relief passed, I really missed her. Even after her stroke, I felt she was "there." I would visit the nursing home and talk to her, try to entertain her. Now she was truly gone.

"When my dad died three months later, my emotions were very different because my father was angry with me—irrationally so. He couldn't forgive me for stepping down from a prominent business position two years earlier. He took it as a personal affront, and spoke to me through clenched teeth. So when he died—after a heart attack in the hospital—my first feeling was deep sorrow because he'd never moved beyond his anger. Later, I was simply glad to have the bur-den of care lifted. It had been a tough four years."

Morgan paused and glanced out his patio door at the golf course fairway behind his large home. I saw him blink rapidly. But his voice was steady when he turned. "You know what I feel today? *Gratitude.* Every time I think about my parents, I'm grateful. They were both bright, healthy people so I have a great genetic inheritance. And though there were a few things that each of them did that I didn't like, they raised me responsibly and with love. I'm forever grateful."

A STEP FORWARD

$\mathcal{J}$f you cared for your elderly parents before their deaths, you, too, may feel as Morgan did—relieved that your burden is lifted. Relief is natural. On its heels will come an inevitable sorrow, and yet, once that passes, many adult children report feeling, as Morgan did: deeply grateful. For the sheer gift of their lives. Somehow, any mistakes their parents made shrink behind the knowledge that their parents did their very best, and gratitude seems appropriate.

Pictures on the Piano

"$\mathcal{J}$'ve turned into my mother," wailed my friend Twila. She swept her arm in the direction of her fireplace mantel. "Family photos all over the place. I remember thinking how absolutely *tacky* it was that my mother kept pictures of all our relatives sitting in frames on our piano. Now I'm doing it."

I smiled. "Me, too."

At some point in life, almost like a primal urge, we start surrounding ourselves with reminders of family, the clan to which we belong, those people to whom we are connected.

Photos sprout like tulips in spring. They hang on family room walls, stair-step from first to second floor, take up space on windowsills, mantels, pianos, television consoles, or bookcases. I call my dining room wall my "ancestors' wall." You can see my parents' bridal portrait, my grandparents' Victorian home, and a wonderful sepia-toned photo of my mother and her siblings as children.

Two of my most prized photos came in the wake of my parents' deaths. One arrived as a gift from my brother Rob six weeks after our father died. It's a casual head shot. Daddy was sitting beneath a tree in the backyard outside Rob's Seattle home. Sun and shade dappled around him. Smile lines creased his eyes. He looked as if he wanted to speak. Rob mounted the photo inside a green mat and carefully framed it.

For weeks after it came, I couldn't bear to hang it on the wall. I wanted it close, and kept it on my desk where now and then I could reach over and touch the glass, as if touching my father. I loved the picture because it was recent and informal—totally unlike the stiff Air Force portraits or the blurry group snapshots I had.

When my mother died, I inherited what looks like an early twentieth century painting of a small, curly-haired angel. All you see is her head and bare shoulders. As a little girl, I thought it *was* an angel until my grandmother explained it was a studio portrait of my mother at age four.

I'm not sure why I particularly love the portrait of my mother at the beginning of her life and the informal view of my father near the end of his. Perhaps it's the different ways in which they took their life journeys. Both pictures have a special hold on my affection, and almost daily, I pause a moment to look at them. Always, I smile.

Award-winning author and motivational speaker BARBARA BARTOCCI lectures frequently on spirituality and self-growth. A presentation trainer for several major seminar companies, Bartocci also serves as a marketing consultant to individual clients. A popular freelance writer for *Woman's Day, Family Circle, McCall's, Good Housekeeping,* and *Reader's Digest*, among others, Bartocci has written three previous books—*Midlife Awakenings, Unexpected Answers,* and *My Angry Son.* Her essays have also been included in several volumes in the *Chicken Soup for Your Soul* series. Bartocci lives in a suburb of Kansas City, Kansas.